David McEvoy

1

Secret Soldiers: Ulster

By David McEvoy

Contents

4

Secret Soldiers: Ulster   Web site.
www.dmcevoy.com

Secret Soldiers: Ulster

By David McEvoy

Preface

I feel that forty years after these events, it's time for me to write them down in order to lay them open to the judgment of posterity. It seems to me to be the appropriate time to allow this narrative and these historic photographs to make their own way into the public domain. In so far as I can, with the aid of material that I have found on the internet and other sources, I have worked in chronological order. Attempting to get all the dates, places, (and names where appropriate) correct. I can only write what I remember and by its very nature this will be my own personal view of these events and how they affected me.

It has been necessary to change the names of certain individuals in order to protect their identities. Particularly with regard to the identities of those people, civilian and military personnel, who were involved in intelligence gathering. I have been advised that a considerable risk to the lives of these individuals still exists. Also, I have taken care in guarding the identities of a close friend and that of two of my former enemies, having learned that sometimes people can make up for the follies of their youth.

Most of these changed identities still retain the original Christian name as well as the first letter of their surname, in order that people who knew them are able to recognise who I am writing about. I have been advised that these changes are, even after all this time, an essential precaution. There is still a great deal that even now, after all these years, I am unable to discuss for both security and personal reasons.

You may well ask why after a silence lasting over forty years, I would choose this moment to acknowledge my involvement in this dark history. My only answer is that the disrespectful treatment I received at a veterans war pension hearing made me think very hard about the values that I have held for most of my life and I decided that the actions of some of the hero's with who I had the privilege to work needed recognition.

I hope that you will find no politically correct platitudes being repeated in this history. I intend to be as open and honest as I can be. Finally, I was recently asked what the difference between a terrorist and a freedom fighter is and yes, I have met both. The main difference between them is that the terrorist forces his view onto the majority by acts of violence or murder perpetrated against them and the freedom fighter simply fights for the values that he or she believes in. I know who I prefer.

Northern Ireland Police Divisions L and M

So Shall They Reap

A young girl, only a child really, watched as the green Morris 1100 approached her. It was travelling along the road through the picturesque Gortin Glen on the outskirts of the Ulster town of Omagh. The child was leading a donkey by its harness along the quiet country road when, suddenly at a hundred yards distance away, dark smoke started pouring from the vehicle as it continued its progress through the tranquil glen. Within a frozen moment in time the moving car exploded in a noisy, pulverising blast, spreading its twisted wreckage over the road and the adjacent fields. The child watched in horror and disbelief as the disintegrating car disgorged the bodies of its three former occupants and draped them in a grotesque tableau along the roads edge and in the surrounding fields.

 It was the morning of Monday June the 25th 1973 and the IRA campaign was into its fourth year. The incidents in the so called border areas had reached their most vicious point with lives being lost on both sides on an almost daily basis.

15 year old Anna Kooke, the young girl who had witnessed this scene of horror, though deeply shocked was physically unharmed, despite the fact that debris from the blast including body parts of the three occupants of the car had been thrown over a large area.

Within half an hour of this grisly scene having been created, I arrived there with the bomb squad. Although some of the fifty pounds of explosives which constituted the bomb had not detonated, enough had gone off to mutilate and rip apart the two IRA volunteers who had been preparing the bomb's timing mechanism on the back seat of the car ready for its target in Omagh, which lay only 1 mile further down the road.

It was customary when a major incident had occurred for "The Gathering" to take place in order to make certain that the scene was left safe and to make sure that any evidence pointing to the perpetrators was collected. The police in the form of Special Branch Inspector Peter Flanagan and Detective Constable John Doherty were the first at "The Gathering". They had already arrived at the scene of carnage and had dragged the three mutilated corpses of the IRA Volunteers together at the side of the road where I was able to inspect and photograph them and record the level of mutilation caused by their mishap. The police were closely followed by Staff Sergeant Ron Beckett and his bomb disposal team, along with two explosive sniffer dogs with their handlers and me. Later the press arrived and were kept at a discreet distance.

The youngest of the three dead men had been driving the car, and had been sheltered to a certain extent from the full effects of the blast by the bodies of his fellow volunteers who we thought to have been crouched over the device, priming it when the detonation occurred. That didn't save him from instantaneous death, but the degree of physical mutilation was far less than with the other two men. I recognised him straight away as Paddy Carty.

As a member of the Army's intelligence section based in Omagh which covered these border areas of Tyrone and Fermanagh, I had taken a particular interest in this young man's blossoming career as a volunteer with "C" Company Mid Ulster Battalion of the Provisional IRA. He was believed to be part of an IRA active Service Unit that had initiated a mortar attack on our base at Lisanelly, just a few days earlier. It crossed my mind that this bomb was heading in the same direction. Paddy Carty was from a republican area of the Tyrone town of Dungannon and it appeared to me that as a result of just one lucky accident we had now seen the back of half of the active service unit to which he belonged. A few months later, Paddy's younger brother would be sent to prison for terrorist offences, confirming for me once again, that these activities often ran in families.

 The two remaining corpses were much more of a problem to identify. One of their heads, although still attached, was in completely the wrong place. An arm and much of the torso was missing. The other body was similarly mutilated and also missing large parts of its torso, but for the moment we were more interested in finding any remaining explosives and fragments of the timing mechanism for clues to its manufacture. It wasn't long before the meat wagon came to remove the bodies to the morgue in Omagh, so after completing the tricky operation of wrapping the mutilated corpses into polythene sheets and placing them in the ambulance, we continued the search for missing body parts.

 The next morning I reported to the intelligence cell as usual to review the newspapers. It had been no surprise to me when I had received the call to the bomb incident the previous day, as I had been working on something that made this attack more than a vague possibility. That morning after working through the Irish papers, one of the lads said. "Hey Dave, have you seen this morning's Daily Express? You're on the front page, mate!" Yes and there it was. I could be clearly seen in the background of a photograph that the paper had taken for its Ulster editions. Front page coverage of the incident, and yes, it was definitely me. I could plainly be seen wearing civilian clothing and holding a camera. This was not supposed to happen, especially not now. Things were already complicated enough without lifting the lid on any part of our shadowy world. How the hell had I got myself into this?

Manners Maketh Man

As a child the words Irish and Catholic were synonymous to me. I was brought up in a devout Catholic family with strong Irish ties and a surname to proclaim it. During my early years my whole life revolved around my family's religious beliefs. The schools that I attended and my social life were all dominated by the Catholic Church. Most of my friends were Catholics and my religion was a comfortable safe blanket for me. Our family were poor. My father worked for low pay in a cotton mill, despite the deformity of his legs, a permanent reminder of childhood rickets. By the time he reached his early forties, he suffered a series of heart attacks and was unable to work again. This left the responsibility of feeding, clothing and housing my older brother and me, to my mother.
My mother was a convert to the Catholic faith. Her parents were of Protestant stock and I can remember her taking some considerable abuse from her father when he lay on his death bed. Nevertheless she stayed faithful to her new religion to her death, which was many years after my father had passed away.

Growing up, in those hungry, deprived years after the Second World War I never felt different to any of my friends. Rationing and shortages was a great leveller. We didn't live in a consumer society and I just accepted that some people had a little more than others. My Catholic upbringing didn't separate me from the other kids on my street. It was more of an addition to my life than an alternative lifestyle. The priority of my loyalties was always, English, British, Irish, in that order and religion came somewhere at the end of the list, and I was intensely proud of all those links. By the time I had finished my soldiering in Ulster I had dropped Irish from the list and never again set foot in a Catholic Church.

When I left school at the age of fifteen I took up an apprenticeship in engineering and within two years I had got my girlfriend pregnant and 'done the right thing' We were both seventeen years of age with a baby boy and fifty shillings per week between us and destitution, so I joined the Territorial Army in order to augment my income. I wasn't ready to settle down, so enjoyed the three years of weekend warfare, until I joined the regular army when I was twenty.

After a year on active service in South Arabia (The Aden Conflict) and a few years in Germany I moved on from tank crewman to Corps HQ policeman. Whilst at the 1st British Corps HQ in Bielefeld I started taking an interest in photography and ended up as a photographer. From which position, it was a small jump to Intelligence.

Background to the Troubles

Ever since the Irish War of independence 1919 - 21 and its subsequent outcome, which was the division of Ireland in 1921, a substantial minority of the population of the country disagreed with the contents of the Anglo Irish Treaty which brought the Irish Free State into being, and left the northern counties as part of the United Kingdom. Within a year civil war had broken out between the pro and anti treaty factions.

Thanks to the military and financial support of their former enemies, the British, the Free State Government won the conflict and brought about an uneasy peace. Certain factions of the IRA though had never accepted this outcome and during the next thirty five years fought three campaigns against both their own government in the south, and the British in the north in order to overturn the treaty and reunite Ireland under their leadership. Somewhere along the line their venom got turned equally against the Northern Protestants culminating in some barbaric sectarian killings during the 1950s border campaign.

By the middle of the 1960s the post civil war divisions had become somewhat blurred and more than a little bit confused. It seemed that politicians within the same parties often held distinctly opposing views on what should have been critical points of collectively held principle.

In the North of Ireland, the majority Protestant population were determined to keep their distance from the activities of their southern neighbours, but there was a tendency for them to react in a predictable and sometimes extreme manner. The population of Ulster was at that time split into approximately one million Protestants and half a million Catholics, with the political divide being along exactly the same lines. The Northern Catholics supported the Social Democratic and Labour Party, (SDLP) and Protestants gave their support to one or other of the Northern Ireland Unionist parties. The Unionists, thanks to their superior numbers held the reins of power and there is no doubt that they used this political muscle to attack the civil rights of the minority Catholic population, by gerrymandering political boundaries, in order to keep political control and manipulating the housing lists and job prospects of the Catholics.

Civil Rights Movement
Therefore in 1968 when the Northern Ireland civil rights movement started up, it gained the support of

many liberal minded Protestants as well as being viewed favourably by many in the UK. It wasn't long though before the true republican nature of this movement would show itself.

The general response to the Civil Rights Association's demands from the Protestant community was one of anger, and many Catholics who found themselves isolated within predominantly Protestant areas had their homes attacked and often burned out by Protestant mobs. Thousands of families felt so intimidated by these events that they moved to what they believed were safer areas or even south to the Republic. The whole population in the north started to polarise in a most divisive manner.

At this point the British government decided that things had gone far enough. They sent in the army in an attempt to defend the hard pressed Catholic communities and try to stop the IRA's movement towards a new campaign in the north, but their actions had been pre-empted by a conspiracy of some highly placed members of the Irish Government. Links had been forged between Irish Army Intelligence and the IRA. The government of the Irish Republic spent over £150,000 on weapons to be sent to Catholics in the north. These negotiations between the IRA and Irish Army Intelligence resulted in the birth of a new, more hard line faction of the IRA to be known as the

Provisional IRA.

The newly formed Provisional IRA had been given to believe that their activities were approved by and supported by the government of the South. It is of course nonsense to state that the conflict was not about religion when virtually everyone on one side was of the Catholic faith and almost everyone on the other side of the conflict was of the Protestant persuasion, although the difference between the two sides was not solely religious. Equally it would be incorrect to look at the problems of 1969 as being the start of these troubles. For many involved it was little more than a continuation of the 1950s Border Campaign which had petered out through lack of interest. These troubles had in fact continued in short bursts ever since the division of Ireland in 1921 when the Protestant dominated northern counties decided against joining the newly formed Irish Free State. For them 'Home Rule' meant 'Rome Rule', and they wanted none of it. Right from 1921 onwards the Republican Movement in Ireland decided to force these Prods in the North to accept what they thought of as domination of the Catholic Church within the Republic, and abandonment of their strong links with the British.

The IRA had no compunction about forcing these changes on their Protestant neighbours at gun point. It is true to say though, that in the early part of the 1969 campaign they initially backed away from committing quite as many purely sectarian murders as they had in the earlier campaigns.

Britain's Shrinking Army

At the end of World War Two, the United Kingdom was left with substantial armed forces including vast numbers of conscripts, with conscription continuing right up to the early 1960s. We had territories across the world which needed defending and policing, as well as it being necessary for us to maintain control of our post war sector of Germany. Our former allies the Russians had, at the end of the war, taken the opportunity to carve out a vast empire in the east of Europe and as Winston Churchill said during his 'Sinews of Peace' address of 5 March 1946, an 'Iron Curtain' had descended across the continent. The whole of Europe was a vast armed camp and many people believed that the unthinkable advent of another world war was hovering just over our horizon.

Hundreds of Soviet tank divisions stood ready in Eastern Germany and Poland to destroy the west and only their fear of a mutually destructive nuclear holocaust maintained the status quo. In 1945 though, the United Kingdom was on its knees. Yes, the war had been won, but at what cost! Our

economy was shattered and it wasn't possible to end all rationing until nine years later in July of 1954. The price tag and sophistication of new weapon systems as well as the perceived need to professionalise the Armed Forces meant that the size of the Army in particular had to shrink at an alarming rate and has continued to shrink ever since. With this much smaller army, our leaders had to find new techniques with which to fight the many 'small wars' that we as a nation, with worldwide responsibilities and commitments, found ourselves embroiled in, whilst keeping our main strength looking watchfully towards Eastern Europe.
The Special Air Service Regiment, who subsequently provided the knowledge and the teeth for most of the army's future clandestine activities had survived these cuts and was still available to be developed into its post war role.

In 1969 Ulster, the campaign of civil disorder rapidly escalated into a fully fledged terrorist struggle causing the British Army to look to its recent past for answers. At this time possibly the most influential voice was that of General Sir Frank Kitson. He had served in most of the counter insurgency operations of the British Army over the previous twenty years, from Kenya in the 1950s, to the Aden Conflict and had became the army's most experienced officer in the field of counter-insurgency and anti-terrorist warfare. The General had recognised early on that if you try to fight terrorists or insurgents in the same way that the military would traditionally fight a war, it would take a vast amount of resources, manpower and equipment and would constitute an unacceptably intrusive burden on the civilian population that the army were trying to protect. Historically, the outcome of such operations had always proven to be bloody and counterproductive in that the application of extreme force is likely to alienate rather than placate the civilian population and that such operations are likely to act as a recruiting Sergeant for the terrorists or freedom fighters. He recognised early that the way to fight fire was with fire.

The British Army had a long history of fighting covert wars, but until Frank Kitson came along the methods and techniques were not formalised and studied as a science. It was not until the late sixties that the army recognised the general's talent and realised that to effectively fight terrorism it was necessary to use the same stealth and gall that the terrorist himself was using.

The key to winning was good intelligence. In simple terms, if you know where a terrorist is going to strike you only need two soldiers at that place to stop him. If you don't know where he will strike you need soldiers on every street corner and in every doorway and you still may not stop him. This dawning recognition started to infiltrate military thinking in a big way from the troubles in Palestine onwards.

The publication of his book *Low Intensity Operations* in 1970 was an important landmark in this progression to a new way of thinking and the General was able to put his theories into action when in 1970 he was appointed as commander of 39th Infantry Brigade in Northern Ireland and was authorised to set up the first (MRF) unit. Kitson created the Mobile Reconnaissance Force, or was it Military Reaction Force, or maybe the Military Reconnaissance Force, or 4 Field Survey Troop Royal Engineers? In fact it was a unit so secret, that I doubt if even they themselves knew who they were. It was his idea to update the concept of Keeny Meeny and add levels of sophistication to it that were unthinkable at its conception during the Kenya uprising and its later adaptation by the SAS during the Aden Conflict.

His idea was to form a military unit that consisted of soldiers and ex terrorists who had been turned and were now working for the army. The nearest units historically to the MRF were the Pseudo-Gangs that the British used by turning them back against the Mau-Mau during their uprising in 1950s Kenya. The MRF's though would have many skills and be classed as Special Forces. They would normally work covertly and in civilian clothing in order to be able to move more freely amongst the general population without being recognised as being soldiers. Thus came into being 4 Field Troop MRF. General Sir Frank Kitson was appointed the Commander-in-Chief UK Land Forces in 1982 and retired at the end of the 1980s leaving a vast legacy.

During the 1969 to 1999 troubles in Northern Ireland there were many agencies involved in the dangerous but very necessary work of gathering intelligence about the plans and activities of the various terrorist groups. MI5 and MI6 as well as the Royal Ulster Constabulary Special Branch were fully committed on the civilian side and the Army had numerous different intelligence gathering assets with the added ability of having a potentially more reactive element to their work.

Both the police and the army, often in unison, were able to respond vigorously and aggressively to incoming intelligence as well as using it to develop more effective use of their resources. In the early part of the campaign there was a certain amount of jostling for position in the intelligence community but it didn't take long for everyone to find their place in the pecking order, and for systems to be devised by which Intel could be properly graded and disseminated, where necessary.

On the other hand the IRA adopted an efficient cellular structure by employing Active Service Units who were supposed to maintain their own personal security. This, in theory helped in the maintenance of its security but in actual fact often hampered the forward transmission of information. In the medium and long term the amount of unnecessary chatter within the republican movement and IRA meant that very little stayed secret for long. Nevertheless these amateurish intelligence gathering systems often had beneficial results for them.

On the British Army's side 14 Intelligence Company, with the help of the SAS, took the lead in covert operations involving surveillance and agent handling. Both 14 INT and its predecessor the MRF or Military Reconnaissance Force used name changing and a deafening silence about its activities to keep its many critics in the dark as to its role. It was often difficult knowing what they were called, never mind what they did for a living! The MRF had in fact come to a sticky end, and had to endure yet another name change when a drive by shooting in Belfast was attributed to them by the Police. On top of which the infamous Four Square Laundry scam blew up in their faces.

The Four Square Laundry

On the 2nd of October 1972 a laundry van trundling through the back streets of republican Belfast came to a halt at yet another stopping point, only to be opened fire upon by a group of men. The attack was organised by the Intelligence Section of the IRA's Belfast Brigade, who afterwards claimed to have killed the driver and two other people inside the van, although that hadn't been the case as the driver was the only casualty. It is difficult to know what undercover operations the army got up to in Ireland, because they had to go wrong in a fairly spectacular manner like the Four Square Laundry scam for the public to get to hear about them at all, and even then reliable detail was scant.

  The British Army had recognised a need to get operatives inside the former no-go areas in order to photograph IRA suspects and gain low level intelligence about the IRA's activities. The infantry, who were constantly mounting roadblocks and other operations in and around the city needed to recognise potential terrorists if they stopped them at a road block. Although this sounds simple enough, it was virtually impossible to move around covertly in those areas. The IRA had scouts everywhere looking out for vehicles or people who didn't belong there, partly because of Prod attacks and partly to keep their movements and activities away from the ever prying eyes of the army. The MRF had to come up with a plan that would allow them to move around freely without arousing suspicion amongst the locals. The plan that they eventually put together was both startlingly simple and incredibly dangerous.

They set up a laundry inside a former no-go area and employed local people to work there. The laundry delivery van had a specially made compartment in the roof space which was large enough to conceal two people. From this hideaway, during deliveries, the operatives would photograph locals at close quarters through special apertures in the body work of the vehicle.

The soiled laundry that the van collected was checked for traces of explosives, firearms residue and blood, as well has being compared by quantity, gender and age to the people who were known to live in the house that it was collected from. For instance, if a lot of men's clothing was coming from a house where an old woman lived alone, they may suspect that the house was being used as barracks accommodation by the IRA and keep a closer watch on it. The MRF had devised a system of tickets and targeted discounts in order to know exactly where the soiled clothing was coming from and be able to target the same address with unbelievable offers in order to get another sniff at their soiled clothing. The whole thing was run by undercover British soldiers, both men and women, with the inadvertent help of locals, including some republicans.

As part of this complex scam the MRF also employed some of their 'Freds' (IRA double agents) in the laundry and this turned out to be their downfall.

A 'Fred' named Kevin McKee had been revealed to the IRA as an informer by another double agent called Seamus Wright. Under torture McKee admitted his involvement with the army and was later executed by the IRA, but not before giving away chapter and verse of the MRFs activities in the former no-go areas. The Laundry's secret was now known by the IRA, who set their local intelligence section to keep surveillance on it for a while to learn about the movement of staff and vehicles. Then, on 2nd October 1972 they struck. The driver of the van, 21 year old Sapper Ted Stuart died instantly in a hail of machine gun fire. Using the same weapon the IRA riddled the roof space of the van and its hidden compartment. The IRA claimed that on the same day they attacked a massage parlour on the Antrim Road which was also being run by an MRF team for intelligence gathering. According to the IRA a total of five undercover soldiers from both sites were supposedly killed, but in the case of the massage parlour, it soon became evident that they had only succeeded in wounding a bystander.

The co-driver of the laundry van on that day, a young female soldier, Lance Corporal Sarah Wake of the Military Police, managed to escape the trap by running to a nearby house claiming that she was being attacked by Prod extremists. She was later awarded a Military Medal and her award was the first to be given to a female by the British Army for undercover work during the campaign. The army only ever admitted to one soldier being killed in this incident and the MRF was never mentioned. Only the soldiers original regiment was given, (all Special Forces soldiers must initially join a normal regiment of the line before undergoing selection and being accepted into a special unit.)

Had it not been for a completely unrelated incident leading to Kevin McKee giving information under torture, the likelihood of the IRA finding out about this audacious prank was minor and it was deemed well worth the risks taken.

The Four Square Laundry Incident is a clear illustration of how some kind of disaster has to occur before the activities of the undercover soldier come under the arc light glare of the public's gaze. Either they get killed in a bodged operation in such a way that the usual cover-up method doesn't work, or are caught out doing something that offends the sensibilities of those members of the public who still think cricket is a gentleman's game. Notable amongst these disasters and according to some people falling into both of the above categories is the killing of Captain Robert Nairac.

Captain Robert Nairac

Robert claimed to be a Military Intelligence Officer but I have also seen him described as the 2nd in command of the highly secretive 14 Intelligence Company (descendents of MRF). His original unit was the Grenadier Guards but by early 1977 he was a highly prized intelligence gatherer and arch proponent of the secret dirty tricks war against the IRA. On the night of 14th of May 1977 he drove out of his base at Bessbrook in his undercover Q car wearing jeans and a duffle coat, looking to the entire world like Danny McAlevey, the Belfast 'Stickie' (IRA Volunteer) that he was going to imitate. He headed straight to The Three Steps Inn in the South Armagh village of Dromintee. The pub was a favourite IRA haunt and a regular gathering place for republicans and this being Saturday night Robert knew that it would be full of Republican supporters.

Robert Nairac was born in Mauritius and had been educated at Ampleforth, an English Catholic public school. He was born into an Anglo Irish family and spent many wonderful holidays as a child in Ireland

where he mastered an uncanny ability to mimic a
number of local Irish accents. On that cold winter
night Robert Nairac had no backup, but that wasn't
unusual for him. He had done this sort of thing many
times before. He was armed only with his Browning
9mm pistol and an amazing courage. The pub was
crowded and a man was singing rebel songs on a
stage at one side of the tatty room. Robert bought
himself a drink and joined in the singing. He didn't
look or sound out of place while he was singing
along with the rebel songs or when he engaged in
conversation with people in the bar, but there was
something about this man that didn't quite ring true.
There were whisperings about Danny, some said
that he was a Provo from Belfast who was on the
run, and others said that they felt uncomfortable
with some of the questions that he had been asking.
Could Danny McAlevey be a spy? The pub was now
crowded, the heating was on and with all those
bodies in close proximity, it had become very hot.
An observant Irishman noted that Robert hadn't
even taken his Duffle Jacket off when, part way
through the evening, he got up on the stage and
started singing *The Broad Black Brimmer*, a
favourite IRA song. The man mentioned his
concerns to others. What if this handsome young
man whom, from his accent was obviously from
Belfast, was a Prod spy working for the Brits?

An argument broke out between Danny and two of

the suspicious locals and when, at the end of the evening, at approximately 11.45 pm, he left the pub a group of men jumped him in the car park. He tried to convince them that he was a Catholic from West Belfast, an active IRA man who was visiting the area. During the struggle his gun fell out of its hiding place in his Duffle coat pocket and bounced along the car park.

A local IRA commander and two IRA volunteers were sent for and the now much larger group of men dragged Captain Nairac off across the nearby border to some woodland in the Republic where his interrogation continued. Robert suffered an appalling fate as he was beaten severely and tortured in the most brutal manner in an attempt to get him to admit to his guilt, but he never varied from his cover story and at one point managed to wrangle his pistol out of the hand of one of his torturers and shoot the man in the leg with it. His vicious interrogation continued throughout the night. The sickening violence that was perpetrated against him left him unable to stand or see properly but at no point did he stop fighting his tormenters. In fact, at one point he managed to relieve the IRA commander of the old revolver that the man had brought with him and was vigorously waving in Robert's face. Robert steadied and aimed the revolver and pressed the trigger only to hear the click as it misfired. Up to nine of them beat him to the ground and retrieved the weapon from his grasp. The end came when his captors tried to trick him by one of them claiming to be a Catholic priest who had come to perform the last rites over his battered body. He was invited to make his confession before meeting God, but even in his battered and bloodied state of a man who was probably close to death, Robert kept to his story. So, convinced that he was a UVF member (Protestant Paramilitary), 24 year old Liam Townson, the local IRA commander, finally dispatched him with a bullet in his head from the revolver that he had brought with him. His first attempt misfired just as it had done when Robert had tried firing it, but the second attempt at firing the gun succeeded and took Roberts life.

It was the following day, when the Army made an announcement, that the IRA discovered exactly who it was that they had executed. Then their propaganda machine went into overdrive, accusing Robert of numerous killings and stating that they had known who he was from the start. According to them he had broken under interrogation and told them about all the highly illegal activities that the army's undercover teams got up to in the province.

Eventually in a Dublin courthouse Townson was sentenced to 13 years in prison. He admitted that Robert had told them nothing and invested Robert Nairac with his lasting epitaph by stating that he was the bravest man he had ever known. Captain

Robert Nairac was later awarded a posthumous George Cross, The citation for which states:

Robert Nairac was subjected to a succession of very exceptionally savage assaults in an attempt to extract information which would have put other lives and future operations at serious risk.
These efforts to break his will failed entirely. Weakened as he was in strength-though not in spirit-by the brutality, he yet made repeated and spirited attempts to escape, but on each occasion was eventually overpowered by weight of the numbers against him.

  Although a few teeth and a quantity of blood was found in the place where he was tortured, the IRA has never disclosed the whereabouts of Robert Nairac's body.

Steak Knife

In time the MRF became 14 Intelligence Company, also known as 'The Det,' which eventually became the United Kingdom's newest special forces regiment called The Special Reconnaissance Regiment or (SRR), which has in some quarters already gained a reputation as the most sinister and secretive arm of the British State.

Britain's Force Research Unit or (FRU) which is believed to be based at Templer Barracks in Ashford, Kent, was thought to have been developed to take over the work of agent handling worldwide. The FRU and its predecessors have done excellent work during their fight against terrorism in the North of Ireland, but there are certain aspects of their activities that I for one find very difficult to accept. Most soldiers would recognise that in order to win, we must all make necessary sacrifices and face dangers. Sometimes it can be crucial to circumvent certain aspects of the law which make the work of our most secret and deadly agents impossible to perform, if adhered to. When a judgment has been made it is sometimes decided that if the enactment of a criminal act by him can keep an agent in place and therefore save many lives in the future, then it must be allowed.

Let us say that it is vital for the army to infiltrate a murderous terrorist organisation such as the IRA in order to gain information about the organisations plans and structure and that the agent to be inserted needs the qualities of loyalty, courage and tenacity as well as certain military skills found commonly amongst serving soldiers.

In order for a new recruit to be accepted within a terrorist group he needs to be able to demonstrate that he or she is both able and willing to commit the most evil offences against other human beings. These crimes against innocent people are unfortunately a necessary part of gaining your terrorist credentials if we agree that it is acceptable to use soldiers or ex soldiers in this way. These recruits, be they male or female would normally need to be of Irish birth and to belong to the same community as the terrorist group, in order for them to infiltrate that group. It stands to reason that they must be given immunity from prosecution for any acts that they have to commit in order to show their credentials in this way, especially if they have been instructed to participate in the commissioning of these acts by their military or Special Branch controller. It surely cannot be right that they should be held liable in a court of law. It must follow that if we use their lives as a resource in order to manipulate and eventually destroy our enemies we must protect and reward them when their work has finished.

I believe that many people would disagree broadly with that kind of generalised comment and for others the complex issues involved would throw up many ambivalent and confused feelings. So to take the scenario a little further, what if, in order to gain the confidence of the terrorists, our infiltrator has to kill innocent people including members of the security forces? What if his controllers allow him to plant bombs? What if he is instructed to execute members of the IRA, believed by the IRA to be informants, in order to protect the integrity of his undercover identity? This may include the execution of people who have infiltrated the terrorist group for the Security Forces.

At this present time the FRU or Force Research Unit are under investigation for some if not all of these kinds of activities, as well as for collusion with Protestant terror groups. In the case of British undercover agents who worked within the IRA, it is true that because of the potentially embarrassing nature of their activities, (which we must remember they were recruited for, often whilst still serving soldiers), these people have in many cases been abandoned and left to fend for themselves in Ireland, under constant threat of discovery by the

IRA and subsequent execution. In fact there may be as many as twenty of these deep cover spies still trapped within the republican movement and ignored by the government of the UK who formerly relied on them so heavily to give it that victory over the IRA.

Possibly the most sinister kind of agent used by the British State against the IRA, was the pure turncoat. Men who started off as true believers in the republican cause joined the IRA and later changed sides to the British for purely financial gain. Some of these attained high positions within the IRA's command structure. For instance, the British agent known as Steak Knife got to the very top of the IRA before being unmasked in 2003 by newspapers in the South of Ireland. At the point where he had to do a runner, he was a close friend of Gerry Adams and was 2nd in command of the Provisional IRA's head butting Squad, who were tasked with the discovery and execution of British spies from within their own organisation. He was thought to be responsible for the killing of many of the IRA's own men who were suspected of having worked for the Brits. If a knock came to the front door of an IRA member, and on opening it he discovered Freddie Scappaticci, he knew that he was about to meet his maker.

Scappaticci's total disappearance after his being revealed as a British spy, left the hierarchy of the Irish Republican Army dazed and confused. Even after he had gone into hiding, the British Army's disinformation campaign made sure that the waters stayed muddied. I read somewhere recently that he is on holiday at Chick Sands in Bedfordshire, where the Intelligence Corps Headquarters are situated. This may be a mischievous joke, but who knows? Maybe it's true!

The British infiltration of the IRA in particular became so thorough that the IRA had little choice but to sue for peace. The Provisional's were able to do little that wasn't either known about in advance, or found out about, including names of perpetrators and vivid details of plans. No one in their organisation could be trusted. Even some members of their leadership had been turned by, or planted by, the British.

This put the army in a difficult position. Should they react to every atrocity that the IRA planned and risk exposing their agents, or should they choose carefully which interventions to make and therefore keep their eyes and ears inside these organisations? Difficult choices had to be made. At the same time the army planned for the future in that they kept alive IRA leaders who showed the right mix of control within the organisation, whilst not holding the most extreme views. These people, the army thought, would be needed later if any kind of a peace was to be negotiated. I personally thought that we should have targeted the whole of their leadership like exterminating a nest of rats. The net result of all this politicking is that the likes of Gerry Adams, Martin McGuinness and other known killers are still at large and earning fat salaries for their political roles, while their victims are left to rot in the dustbin of history.

Unbelievably though, I can say one thing in favour of the IRA, and that is that they took far better care of their veterans than our government did for our brave soldiers.
In the event though the building blocks of peace were knocked down time after time, due to there being so many people with a vested interest in keeping the slaughter going. Vast amounts of money and prestige were shared out amongst the combatants on both sides of the conflict, but particularly the republican side. Many of those involved were little better than gangsters and to disagree with them or to speak out against them, often resulted in death. Many of these killers are still walking the streets of Ireland today.
There is no need for us to feel guilty about the way in which the IRA was finally defeated. Of course the British government as per usual managed to snatch defeat from the jaws of victory! By allowing the sanctimonious Eire government into the decision making process. It is right and proper that the Catholic community of the north should gain their

full rights and representation from the outcome, but it is sick that the terrorists in the form of Sinn Fein, which is the IRA's political wing, should end up strutting around Stormont, and doing so whilst keeping up the sickening pretence that they were anything other than murdering scum.

The Tour

A normal tour in Ulster lasted four months but The First Royal Tank Regiment's (1 RTR) tour in 1973 was for eighteen months and was accomplished during the worst part of the '69 to 2003 troubles. Furthermore, the tour took place in one of the most troubled areas of Northern Ireland. Most lists of incidents that took place during The Troubles will, (when it comes to the border areas of Fermanagh and Tyrone), simply highlight the most serious incidents and cover the rest by stating "too many to list." During 1RTR's stewardship of these areas, which included 53 percent of the border with the Republic, there were literally hundreds of incidents, from mass murder through indiscriminate bombings and intimidation, to murderous full scale attacks.

The Ulster Defence Regiment (UDR) became operational in 1970. This new regiment was made up from part time members of the local community and was the largest regiment in the British Army with seven battalions. Later in 1992 the regiment, which had, by then eleven battalions, amalgamated with the Royal Irish Rangers and became the Royal Irish Regiment.

Together with the 350 or so soldiers of the 1st Royal Tank Regiment, the 4th and 6th UDR battalions constituted the main backup for the Royal Ulster Constabulary in Fermanagh and South Tyrone in 1973 and 1974. Throughout the campaign the men and women of these two UDR battalions acted with great courage and lost many soldiers to the bombs and bullets of the IRA. As a whole, over 200 UDR soldiers were killed on active service during the troubles with more than 60 of their veteran's murdered after completion of service. The total number of the UDR's casualties including injured must be well into the thousands.
The work that the regiment, who were all locally recruited did, was invaluable. But these important day to day duties often fell into the category of prevention rather than direct action against the IRA and therefore the number of IRA members killed by the unit was relatively low.

Never the less the "Provos" seem to have held a pathological hatred for the UDR, which resulted in members of the regiment being targeted in large numbers. You could be forgiven for thinking that this hatred was linked to the fact that the regiment was predominantly made up from Protestants? But of course that can't be so, as we were always told that religion played no part in the troubles: Bit of a mystery that.

In the early days of its formation a much larger percentage of the UDR came from the Catholic community. This didn't suit the republican movement at all, so they put an end to it by targeting Catholic members and made it impossible for all attempts at religious diversity to succeed. Most of the members of that brave regiment performed their duties in an even handed way, when dealing with their Catholic neighbours as with the Royal Ulster Constabulary. Some courageous Catholics refused to be dictated to by the paramilitaries, often losing their lives as a consequence.

I was part of the army's intelligence element and found that in these early days of the campaign, we were to some extent developing our techniques as we went along. Our task was 'The Collection, Collation and Dissemination of intelligence.' To this end we did everything from reading the newspapers to covertly photographing terrorist suspects, from interrogation and surveillance, to dirty tricks. Anything short of open criminality was acceptable. If you crossed the line you kept it to yourself and only referred to it indirectly amongst others in the know. The fact that even our superiors often had little idea exactly what our role was or what we got up to, added to a feeling of freedom of action.

We were fighting an enemy who had plenty of

backing in the UK, from pink liberals and naive do-gooders. The IRA and friends were quick to scream "martyr" whenever any of their number were killed during operations. But we fought on, usually with one hand tied behind our backs by the twin shackles of political correctness and foolish regulation from our masters. During a campaign that lasted twenty seven years, the IRA never once captured a soldier or police officer without torturing and murdering him. Yet they still had the sickening gall to complain bitterly when volunteers were ambushed and killed during their murderous attacks against unarmed off-duty UDR soldiers who were perhaps delivering milk or going about their normal daily lives. They even had the unmitigated effrontery to make reference to the Geneva Convention during some of their nauseating tirades and more recently I have heard of attempts to gain compensation by some of their families. This would be a sick joke were it not for the fact that our morally crippled government are likely to consider some of these demands if the Good Friday agreement comes under pressure from further acts of terrorism.

Bizarrely it was illegal for us to collect information about people, even those in communities that were supporting the terrorists that we were trying to fight. In the UK it was classed as collecting a census and therefore illegal under British law for anybody other than the government to do. Yes we did collect information about huge numbers of people, but it was done covertly in order not to offend the sensibilities of the IRA's political allies. A series of governments of varying political persuasion continued to reinforce this nonsensical situation. What other country in the world would expect the cream of its youth to sacrifice itself in such a sickeningly futile manner on the altar of political correctness?

In those days there were no such things as personal computers. At first the vital information that we gathered was written on easily lost pieces of paper, and much of this information was simply remembered. Of course when our intelligence turned out to be particularly important it was dispatched to brigade to be entrusted to their main frame computer. Towards the end of 1973 our systems were updated, and we thought, brought bang up to date by the addition of a Cardex system.

The way the system worked was that each of our potential terrorists had a unique card. Information was written on that card. Some distinctive or useful bits of information about the target were accompanied by a punched hole on one edge of the card, the position of which corresponded with the holes for that type of information on the cards of other targets. So when all the cards were placed in the special box provided, we were able by means of a metal rod through the relevant holes (which were meant to line up) to extract all the cards in the database which corresponded with one particular feature. When a card did not hold this particular information its edge would have a space where the rod was able to move without extracting the card. For instance within seconds we were able to find all the targets who drove red cars. Compared with what had gone before this new system was quite useful but very limited. I spent hours viewing photographs of suspects. If I was in the Intelligence Cell and had nothing else to do I would thumb through book after book of photographs of suspects, familiarising myself with their faces. This time spent was to be well rewarded during the months that followed, as twice I recognised potential terrorists' by this means alone.

One of the things that I learned very early on was that the so called 'Republican Movement' didn't give a fig for the truth. Their literature was full of imaginary torture of IRA prisoners, as well as other reprehensible acts, most of which were complete nonsense. On one occasion when I had returned to Lisenely after having delivered a prisoner to the RUC station in Omagh, I was asked if I would take a phone call from a priest called Father Denis Faul who was enquiring about the welfare of the man who had been arrested. The prisoner's farm had been searched as a result of information from an informer, and a large quantity of arms and explosives had been found hidden in his garden and fields.

I had heard of Denis Faul, he was what I classed as an IRA priest. He was immensely concerned about the welfare of captured terrorist suspects but took little or no interest in the welfare of their victims. Whenever a volunteer was picked up by the army, Denis Faul or another priest with IRA sympathies kicked up an unholy fuss about torture and abuse. In this case, as in most others his allegations were completely untrue. But Father Faul like so many before and after him assumed an inside knowledge and was exempt from all reason. He spat a list of lies and deceit at me and wouldn't listen to any of my explanations. Nothing that he said to me bore any resemblance to the facts. In the end I put the phone down on him and muttered "fuck off" as I went back to my coffee. Of course Father Faul's belligerent, blinkered attitude helped him to fare well amongst Ireland's Catholic hierarchy. I believe he ended up as Monsignor Denis Faul.

I found myself responsible for prisoners on a number of occasions and I can state that none of them were ever treated with anything other than distant courtesy by me or any other person whilst I was present. The nearest thing to abuse that I ever saw in Ulster, was when a prisoner was beaten up during his capture. If you consider that when first sited he was carrying a powerful assault rifle and had been laid in ambush to kill soldiers with a massive bomb, his beating, though thorough, was very brief and an understandable reward for his attempted murder. The soldier who chose to tackle this armed terrorist, instead of shooting him, was probably high on adrenalin and possibly still in fear for his own life at the moment of the assault. Unlike the IRA, British soldiers didn't do torture. At the same time it is the duty of our political masters not to hamstring our activities in such a way as to be supporting the conduct of our enemies whilst leaving us no legal way of striking back.

The full role of some members of the Catholic clergy is now just starting to emerge. Priests such as Father James Chesney, who died in 1980, had been involved in terrorist activities. Father Chesney's involvement along with others was deemed so divisive that a conspiracy was cooked up between the then British secretary of state for Northern Ireland, William Whitelaw and Cardinal William Conway, who was the head of the Catholic Church in Ireland. Both the government of the UK and the church in Ireland were, it seems, desperate to hide any evidence that pointed to the conflict having a basis in religious differences.

The 1972 triple bombing at the centre of these allegations took place in the small town of Claudy on July the 31st 1972. There was no warning given and nine people including a girl of nine died when the three car bombs exploded. The victims of this atrocity, which was one of the worst in the whole campaign, comprised of 4 Catholics and 5 Protestants.

Father Chesney's involvement in the bombings was hushed up and he was transferred to the Irish Republic by the church, to a new parish at Malin Head in the border county of Donegal. His new parish was easily close enough to Ulster for him to have carried on his activities by the then popular cross border methods. According to the Police Service of Northern Ireland *(post Good Friday Agreement police service)*, who have been looking into the often repeated allegations, this move took place shortly after and as a direct consequence of the written contacts between "Willy Whitewash" and "Willy Conaway". Apparently the general public in the UK and Ireland didn't possess the maturity to deal with the facts as they really were, or this man against whom there was a huge amount of evidence, would have died in prison as he deserved.

Isn't it time that the church came clean about members of its clergy who were involved in the troubles? I for one think so. According to Sean O Callaghan in his excellent book *The Informer* there were other priests involved in both the training and on the military side of the IRA.

The republican movement published several news

sheets, which they used for propaganda. Some of their claims against the army and police were laughable and beyond belief. On occasions I read their distorted claims about operations in which I had either taken part or had inside knowledge. Their lies and deceptions were only too happily believed by their readership, and usually quoted as proven truths.

Omagh

Omagh itself was a deceptive kind of place. It had a Catholic majority, and the kind of 50/50 religious balance that in other parts of Ulster often meant riots and tension. Omagh's population usually appeared relatively friendly. It was no problem for soldiers and their families to go shopping in the town or even go for a drink in most of the excellent pubs. All the streets leading to the town centre were blocked off, some semi permanently as part of the security cordon, and others by means of manned checkpoints. These basic precautions by the police and UDR made certain that no bombs could get through to the main shopping street, or so we thought. Despite the fact that the system was by no means foolproof, it did give a much greater feeling of security and made it much more difficult for the IRA to plant their bombs. Although there were many republican supporters in the area, the local IRA in early '73 was of the old school, and generally acted out the roles of reconnaissance and support rather than direct action. Volunteers were usually sent in from other areas to commit acts of terrorism, whilst the local heroes bragged and sang songs about it. The areas surrounding Omagh and Tyrone itself, was a different matter. The army's encounters with locals would often more accurately be classed as confrontational.

Our small Intelligence cell, which fluctuated in number at around six men, was based at Lisenely Barracks on the outskirts of the town, with outposts at Killeter County Tyrone and Saint Angelo, a large fortified compound on an airfield in County Fermanagh. Omagh's position as county town of Tyrone made it one of the centres for services such as policing and the fire brigade. There was a large regional hospital and it was the centre for local government. All in all, Omagh, though comparatively small, stood out as a target for both the IRA and other extremist groups. Large parts of both Tyrone and its neighbour Fermanagh were classed by us as border areas and most of the atrocities that were committed there had some degree of cross border stratagem involved.

By 1973 the government of the Irish Republic, who in the early days of the campaign had secretly encouraged the IRA with promises of help and support, and had even intimated military support from the Irish Army, came to their senses, in that they started half-hearted co-operation with the British. It was the realisation that they were becoming more vulnerable themselves to the somewhat crackpot ebb and flow of Irish politics and their recognition of the increasing criminal gangster direction that the IRA was taking. They began verbally condemning the violence of the IRA but at the same time they did very little in real terms to stop the export of death across their borders and the Irish Sea to Britain. In fact, although elements of the Irish Special Branch did good work in controlling the activities of the IRA within their own borders. The Irish state didn't give, 'a stuff,' as long as their own population didn't have to suffer at the hands of these lunatics.

The IRA in order not to upset the Irish government too much and cause them to crack down would often, when murdering people in the Republic, drag their bodies across the border into the north. Or take them across on foot before executing them, thus giving the impression of a peaceful Republic.

The Knock-na-moe Castle Hotel, which is now an upmarket housing complex stood in its own extensive grounds in the countryside on the outskirts of Omagh. A large neo-gothic structure, it looked as if it had been converted to a hotel from a substantial country house. The hotel was popular across the religious divide, but in those days was a hotbed of IRA activity. Every Friday night a dance was held and on the night of Friday the 18th of May, Derek Reed, an army helicopter pilot attended. Once inside, Derek met up with three other pilots from the helicopter squadron and an army recruiting sergeant from the careers office in the town. The crowd inside wasn't as great as they would normally have expected it to be but there was still a fair few people in attendance. If the men had questioned the significant drop in the venues expected attendance, it may well have saved their lives. But they didn't and in the early hours of the following morning when the dance finished, and after having a good night out, the five climbed into Derek's car in the car park. The car exploded as it started to move away. Sergeants Derek Reed, Barrie Cox, Sheridan Young and Fred Drake were killed instantly. The fifth man, Sergeant Arthur Place, who was driving the car died in hospital a few days later. A fifty-pound booby trap bomb had been placed under the car during the course of the evening. There were suspicions that later emerged of a possible IRA 'honey trap' operation. But it was subsequently decided that it was unlikely that the IRA would risk its female volunteers in so obvious a prank. Nevertheless the possibility was looked at very seriously for some time.

There was a feeling of stillness the following morning as I entered the Headquarters building for my first day with the Omagh intelligence section. I had arrived in Omagh the previous afternoon having travelled by ferry from Liverpool to Belfast and onwards to Omagh by bus. Although I was a serving soldier the work I did made it necessary for me to wear civilian clothing at all times. I sauntered through the Headquarters building and up to the Operations Room on the first floor to where the Intelligence Cell was located. The room was small with a security locker at one end in which we were to keep our weapons. There were desks positioned around the outside walls for people to work at, so I commandeered a desk located mid way along a wall with a low window that gave me a view of the road outside the headquarters building, and down to the guard room at the main gate of the camp. Not all of the section members had arrived on station yet so I had pretty much the choice of everything. The captain who was our Intelligence Officer (IO) suggested that I start by picking up my weapon from the arms store and familiarise myself with the camp. He informed me that a serious incident had occurred during the previous night in which four soldiers had been killed and one was seriously injured and that I was likely to be needed later as part of the crash out team.

The arms store was located near to the camp's main gate and guard room. I took a walk down and asked the armourer for my weapon, which, once booked out would stay permanently with me. I thought he was joking when he presented me with a large ancient revolver. In answer to my demand of "what the fuck's that!" and "how am I supposed to hide that under my jacket," he explained that there was a shortage of suitable hand guns in the army at the time. As with most situations that our political masters sent us into it was a matter of act first and think afterwards. I was assured that as soon as a Browning pistol became available, I would be first in line for it. On the way back to RHQ I collected my six rounds of ammunition from the ammunition store, which is always kept separate from the Arms Store and loaded my gun in the specially provided loading bay. The sand filled enclosure that made up the loading bay was intended to catch any accidental discharge of weapons during the loading procedure. From now on, whenever I was in the safe area of camp I would store my gun along with its ammunition in the intelligence cells security locker, for speed of access, rather than returning it to the arms store after every use.

Most of the small group of men gathered in the cell that morning knew each other well. All of us were wearing casual civilian clothes and were being addressed by a slightly overweight man who was standing next to a massive German shepherd dog, which I discovered had the bad habit of pinning its victim to the wall while it towered over them and mercilessly licked their faces. On this occasion the dog remained passive as his master briefed the group on the latest situation in and around the volatile county of Fermanagh. Apparently the man, who had the rank of Major, was the Military Intelligence Officer for police division "L" which covered that county. I quickly realised that it was going to take some time before I became familiar with the tactical situation. The area that we controlled was vast, nearly 1800 square miles, and the many Gaelic town and village names had not yet found their place on my mental map of the area. When he had finished his briefing his place was taken by another officer who introduced himself as the MIO for police division "M" (South Tyrone). Mike Mullen, whom I later discovered was a Captain from the Royal Anglian Regiment quickly showed himself to be a first class intelligence officer. He was astute and always had his finger on the pulse.

I later discovered that Mike had a habit of turning up, as if by magic, in the oddest places when things were about to go ballistic. But at this time he struck me as being in his early thirties, about 5ft 8in with a pleasant round face and long blond hair and he spoke informatively about the military situation in the southern part of Tyrone where we were based. The job of these officers was to act as an intelligence link between the regular army in their assigned areas and any special forces operating there as well has the Royal Ulster Constabulary's Special Branch and mainly part time, Ulster Defence Regiment. Each police division in Northern Ireland had its own MIO. The others present were, Davy (Jock) Steele a

talented folk singer. Paddy Carrol, a short lean
soldier from Liverpool and best mate of Davy Steele
and George Mandaracus, who we all knew as Randy
Knackers, more so because it rhymed with his Greek
surname than to any masculine activity on his part.
Randy Knackers appeared to view his own role in
the Int cell as office manager. Lastly there was Ben
Campbell, a friend that I had known for a number of
years.

In my case it soon became apparent that I fell
somewhere outside everyone's orbit. As long as I
showed up in the Int Cell from time to time and
made myself available for any tasks that any of the
IOs had for me, I was able to pick and choose my
own operations to get involved in. The consequence
of which was that I got involved in everything that
was happening. So when the briefing was complete,
and I had learned that there had been an incident
the night before and that personnel were needed to
collect evidence at the scene I thought I might as
well get stuck into the tour so off I went.

On arrival at the hotel where the incident had
taken place, I was told by one of the dog handlers
that the bodies of the victims had been removed,
(the bits that they could find anyway). I spent the
remainder of this inauspicious day collecting
fragments of car, clothing and people into bin liners.
The trees surrounding the car park were draped by
the remnants of the explosion including human flesh

and body parts. I suppose that first day at work should have told me something about the next eighteen months.

As the days and weeks passed by I fell into a routine. Each day I reported to the intelligence cell to read the Irish papers, both local and national. It was a job that we all did if we were available. A matter of many hands made light work of a necessary, but boring task. A great deal of low grade intelligence was gleaned from this source. It also helped in building up background knowledge and giving us an unbiased view of the situation. If there were incidents I would make myself available to accompany the bomb squad or the police to the scene. Some days I would be tasked to do a job by either one of the two Military Intelligence Officers, or by our Intelligence Officer.

This work was often of a photographic reconnaissance, or surveillance nature which I sometimes accomplished along with other Intel people, but more often than not I did it on my own. All the members of the 'Int' section always of necessity wore civilian clothing, and were able to bypass much of the normal military dress and discipline code. Our weapons as previously stated, were kept in the Intelligence Cell for ease of access. We needed them night and day at very short notice, therefore when in camp we kept them in a security locker within the intelligence cell, which was out of bounds to everyone but operations staff. In order to maintain our covert capability, a weapons system that could be concealed in our civilian clothes was necessary.

The 9mm Browning pistol was our favoured weapon of choice. Mike Mullen carried a 9mm Walther PPK and for a short time I was lumbered with that bulky Webley revolver which was difficult to conceal and difficult to retrieve from its hiding place. The Webley supposedly went out of service in the early 60's, but because the army were short of hand guns, they resurrected a few of them in the early part of the IRA campaign, despite having very little ammunition for them. The Army also didn't, at that time, supply holsters for covert weapons, so we had to come by our own. I was able to acquire mine by negotiation with a young lad who was doing a solo evening shift at a local shoe factory. The shoulder holster was made to measure for me and I insisted on paying its helpful creator with a small financial reward. I soon discovered that the shoulder holster was bulky and difficult to conceal, so when, on leaving, someone bequeathed me a small belt holster that was worn on the inside of the wearers belt. I found that positioning the new holster on my left hip with the hand grip facing forward was for me the best practical solution, so I stuck with it until the end of my service. Within a few weeks my ancient Webley had been exchanged for the better suited Browning pistol.

During the next few days I took what opportunities I could to accompany the bomb disposal team whenever they were called out. Notably on the 26th May over one ton of illegal explosives grade fertiliser was found at Beragh by Sgt Dave Ross of A Sqn. We moved this enormous cache to the middle of a field and blew it up. On the same day a large quantity of ammunition and explosives were discovered by assault troop "A" Sqn at Derrygonnelly. So when we had finished at Beragh we drove to the new location and disposed of all the explosives in the same way. This find included Gelignite, Sulphate of Ammonia, packets of Plaster Gelatine, and several metres of Blue Sump Fuse and some Sulphate of Ammonia. There was also a quantity of assorted rifle and pistol ammunition. One arrest was made and I escorted the prisoner to Omagh RUC station.

Two days later on the 28th May, a bomb made up of 80 lb of commercial explosives demolished the new Head Quarters of 4 UDR at Lisnaskea. The new building was next to the police station and surrounded by civilian housing and still had forty men working on its construction. A short warning was given before the (Semtex) went off causing extensive damage to the building but no injuries. The amount of damage done to the building was way out of scale with the size of the bomb that had been laid. This was due in part to the placing of the device and in part to the fact the explosives used were top grade commercial plastic explosives. There was a strong possibility that this device had been secreted on to the site by one of the men still involved in the construction work.

I had arranged for myself to be billeted with the Bomb Squad in order to be sure of being in the know when they were called out during silent hours. It was important that I went with them to glean as much intelligence as possible about both the modus operandi of the bombers and their method of manufacturing of those devices. Later in the year my self-appointed task was taken on by a newly formed Bomb Intelligence unit of the Royal Military Police, consisting of two properly trained non commissioned officers. Their task being to gather and collate all the relevant information and evolving specification of the Improvised Explosive Devices, (bombs) as our Ammunition Technical Officer (ATO) dealt with them. Under the leadership of our ATO we were slowly bringing a more professional feel to the bomb business. Much of my time was spent on other assignments, away from bomb disposal, but it was always a great feeling of belonging when I was back with the Bomb Squad.

Because of the danger involved in the work that they did, the ATOs only completed a short tour of about three months before being replaced with 'new meat'. The ATOs team faced many of the same dangers as he did and were all volunteers from different regiments, most of them staying with the team for the full tour. Our new ATO, Staff Sergeant Ron Beckett, took over from his departing comrade in late June. Ron was a pleasant, friendly man with an easy going disposition, nothing fazed him and everyone liked him. He even managed to put some fun back into what was an uncomfortably serious business. Ron was a family man with a Father Christmas personality.

His first call out was to another bomb at the Knock-na-moe Castle Hotel. A suspicious car had been found in the car park of the hotel, only yards from where the five soldiers had been killed just a few weeks earlier. Ron Beckett and his team were called to the scene, and as usual I was with them. There were a number of cars parked immediately in front of the Hotel and it didn't take long to detect where the stench of the home made explosive ANFO was coming from. The source of this powerful odour was a dark coloured saloon car parked next to the hotel's main entrance. Ron, who was a much less overtly careful man than his predecessor, wanted some photographs of the scene while deciding how he would deal with it. So I took some shots from the car park and then, at Ron's request, climbed a fire escape onto the roof of the hotel in order that I could position myself directly above the suspect car for more photographs. There was nothing else to see! It was, I thought, too big a risk to take in order to simply gain a close up photograph of nothing, but Ron was the boss at the scene of a bomb and I liked and respected him. It crossed my mind that if the bomb went off I would become a permanent part of the local landscape, but my climb was uneventful and I was able to get the photographs that were needed. I was less than impressed as to the logical reasoning behind me risking my life to gain photographs of what was to all outward appearances, just a car.

From the outside this car looked exactly what it was, a somewhat tatty, ordinary saloon car. All the explosives were crammed into the locked boot of the vehicle. Bombs were often timed to go off when they were being worked on in order to kill the ATO or members of his team. When I had moved away to a safer distance from the car, Ron started work on it by firing five rounds of 12 bore solid shot at its boot from a pump action shotgun that we always carried with us. Although these rounds were passing completely through the car's body work, it soon became apparent that we would be unable to observe the effect that this approach was having on the bomb inside. So a different method of disruption was decided upon which we knew as the 'Segmented Plate' method. The trouble was that having now already disturbed the bomb, there was a heightened chance that it would 'cook off' while it was being worked on. But hey ho, nothing fazed Ron very much and he just carried on setting up his Segmented Plate within inches of the car.

The Segmented Plate was a strange device. If you can imagine a light metal stand holding a vertical steel plate and the front of the plate has attached to it a kind of frame. Resting loosely in the frame was a sandwich of plastic explosive and a one inch thick segmented steel plate. The idea being that the frame was propped against the area of the car where the bomb had been placed. In this case the method of detection was nothing more sophisticated than Ron using his nose to sniff around the car to indicate the bomb was positioned in the boot. On detonation the steel backing plate allowed the explosive force to travel in only one direction, forward and through the car boot, carrying the segments of the plate with it. The effect was similar to a giant shotgun being fired at the car from very close range. The segments of the 1 foot square steel plate drove through the bodywork of the car disrupted the timing mechanism and detonator of the bomb as it passed through and left a large ragged hole through which the bomb was exposed.

On this occasion it worked without setting off an explosion in the car but instead resulted in igniting a fire in the boot which was fuelled by the diesel oil which was a component of the bombs make up. The lack of an explosion was a particularly helpful conclusion as the bomb's detonation would have resulted in the destruction of the whole building and could possibly have killed some of us as well, because in my opinion we were too close to the bomb. Then with the help of the fire brigade's high-pressure hoses, the fire was extinguished and the remaining explosive was safely washed out of the car. The bomb was calculated to contain three hundred pounds of ANFO (high nitrate fertiliser and diesel oil) with a primer of CO-OP (made from animal feed sugar) and was quite large enough to have destroyed everything for a hundred yards around. As we worked on the bomb our thoughts were with the five soldiers who had been killed in that very same car park just a few weeks previously. The bomb that killed them was only one eighth of the size of the bomb that we were now dealing with.

When the majority of the explosives had been washed out, we hitched the ruined vehicle up to one of our armoured cars and dragged it to the far end of the car park where the clean-up operation was completed. The car was then handed over to the scenes of crime team from the Omagh police. At that point the ATO team headed back to Lisanelly Camp which was only a mile or so down the road and prepared for their next call out. Walking down to the town centre I met up with Davy Steele, another member of our intelligence section, to carry out a security survey of central Omagh.

In order to be sure that a small town like Omagh was safe from the threat of terrorist bombings it was necessary to put yourself into the same mindset as the terrorist. It is only possible to guard solely pedestrian areas with any realistic degree of success. Even then a small bomb can be carried into the cordoned area by a determined terrorist. Every legitimate means of entry for vehicles into the cordoned areas of the town, as well as other ways that an entry might be forced, must be looked at and assessed in our struggle to give the security forces a chance of keeping these areas relatively free from attack.

This task is made more difficult by the nature of those areas that are to be specially defended. Often they are full of shops and offices which will need vehicular access in order to make necessary deliveries. Measures can be taken to defend other, non cordoned areas, but our expectation of success in these is usually less. Therefore it was our task to assess all the possibilities and for others to make decisions on practical, as well as political and economic grounds.

The Honey Trap

In the aftermath of the murder of the five soldiers at the Knock-na-moe Castle Hotel, the general consensus was that they were caught in a classic honey trap. There was some speculation in the local and national papers, and amongst the military, that local girls were involved in enticing these men to their deaths. Special Branch, in the person of Inspector Peter Flanagan, was in fact convinced that this was the case. One girl in particular was under suspicion. She was known to have met Sgt Reed, the owner of the doomed vehicle before the night of the killing, and she also had the required paramilitary links to make her a top suspect. Of course knowing something in Northern Ireland and proving it were two very different matters. I decided with this in mind to make a point of trying to meet up with this suspect.

As a security measure off duty soldiers were occasionally limited to camp or quarters areas with little or no notice. The idea being that this cut down on their predictability of movement. It became more difficult for the Provo's to plan attacks against soldiers who went to the local pubs for a drink. For the same reason individual pubs were put out of bounds for short periods and some on a permanent basis. Intelligence soldiers frequently visited the favourite squady haunts, and always carried a concealed weapon for their own defence. As stated, members of the intelligence cell did whatever they could to blend in with the local population without being recognisable as soldiers and when out of camp always travelled armed with a personal weapon concealed in a shoulder or hip holster.

Our armed visits to pubs and restaurants in Omagh and any of the other towns near to bases gave added security to the off duty personnel. It was in the Silver Birch Hotel on Gortin Road on a night when troops were restricted to camp that I first met up with Deirdre MacDaill, or as most people knew her, Sinead. She was small in stature, about 5ft 2in tall and slim, weighing little more than 7 stone and dark brown hair. At twenty four years of age she was feminine and attractive. Sinead was the girl who had been involved with one of the dead pilots that were blown up in the car. Sinead was discussed a lot in intelligence circles and she was cynically labelled Miss Carrickmore, this being a reference to her undoubted beauty and a tongue in cheek dig at her deeply republican home village. She spent many hours under questioning by the Royal Ulster Constabulary Special Branch after the bombing and rightly so. Night after night Sinead was picked up and questioned, but to no avail about the murder of the five pilots. Whether she was an involved in that incident was an unlikely possibility, but in every other way we believed her to be mixed up at the deepest level with the IRA.

The pub was empty as I walked up to the bar and ordered my drink. Sinead was the only other customer there and had obviously come to meet someone. I recognised her and said, "Hello." "Where is everybody tonight?" she replied, glancing around the room, to which I confirmed that there was a curfew in place, and that whoever she had come to meet was more than likely stuck in camp. We sat and talked, and she came across as being an intelligent, confident young woman. Apparently she was a nurse and married to a British soldier in Germany. They were on the point of divorce and she was on an extended visit to her family, who lived in one of the villages in the staunchly republican Carrickmore area of Tyrone. She didn't question the fact that I was able to visit the pub when the other military personnel were restricted to camp, and made no comment about my appearance; hair, beard, etc, that was not what you might expect of a soldier. My impression of her was that she liked to take risks and that to her I constituted a dangerous challenge. After a couple of hours we went our separate ways promising to meet again. After that brief encounter I realized I was strongly attracted to Sinead, I found her exciting and sexy. She made no bones about her allegiances but somehow I felt that on a personal level, I was able to trust her. I wanted more of this woman even though my main motivation was to destroy all that she apparently stood for. Her strong republican beliefs meant that I was totally opposed to every value that she held close. Above all her support for the IRA made her an enemy. I had arranged to meet her again on the Saturday evening.

The following day was Monday the 5th June, during the course of the day the IRA killed two people in our area of responsibility. A 17 year old Catholic called Terence Herdman was shot dead in retaliation for allegedly being an informer for the security forces. None of us who attended the scene of his execution had ever heard of this young man. Maybe he was a Tout, (informant) and maybe he wasn't - who knows! His killing took place near the village of Clogher in County Tyrone. On the same day a 22 year old Royal Ulster Constabulary police officer called David Purvis was shot from a passing car whilst on foot patrol, he was left to die on Bellmore Street in Enniskillen, County Fermanagh. I wasn't able to attend the scene of constable Purvis' murder as I was already tied up at the scene of the other killing. The remainder of that week went by fast, a lot was happening. I attended the disposal of

2 large bombs with ATO and spent a lot of time catching up on paperwork.

When Saturday eventually came along, I was, to say the least, surprised when Sinead turned up for our meeting. In actual fact I had thought of little else except her since we last met. I ordered drinks and we sat down in a corner of the Silver Birch. The bar where we met had seen better days and was part of a rundown hotel complex. It was a single story structure situated on the Gortin Road just outside Omagh and close to the camp. In front of the bar, and visible through the large windows, was the laughably titled car park, its irregular surface covered with some kind of cinders. Sinead had arrived in a dark blue Mini Clubman, which I later discovered to be her pride and joy. I had watched her walk from her car into the doorway of the hotel and kept a particular eye on the car park for other vehicles, in case this turned out to be a setup. But she had entered the bar and walked straight to me and we were now sitting with our drinks. With hardly a word spoken, she looked me straight in the eye and sarcastically accused me of being a snooper. It was obvious that she had made enquiries about me during the intervening days.

"I'm not prepared to talk about anything military with you," was my only comment.

"Well I've had quite enough of you bastards over the last few weeks," she replied. "Can't you fuckers leave me alone."

I was thinking to myself that this was spiralling out of control, and was there any point in carrying on with it? Then out of the blue she said. "Shall we go somewhere else?" and after a slight pause I answered. "Yes."

I woke up in camp early the next morning with the scent her perfume and the softness of her hair caressing my face. It was a trick of my imagination, I was alone. We had driven in her car for a while and then stopped on a quiet country road. We sat there talking for what seemed like hours. I knew enough about this woman to recognise that she was deadly, but there was also a powerful, if fragile courage there. She was the possessor of a nature that was both gentle and fierce. But the thing that really stood out was control.

Even if I hadn't known it already, last evening's discussions would have left me with little doubt that she was at least on the fringes of the IRA. She had been involved in the Civil Rights movement in its early days and there was a strong feeling that this lady was prepared to fight like hell for the things that she believed in. Knowing that I was becoming emotionally entangled with her and even though prepared to accept that we were probably in opposing armies, I was falling for her. But if people were right about her involvement in the murder of the five army pilots, I couldn't accept the depth of treachery that it would take to commit such an act.

For someone to befriend another human being, in order to take their life, was for me, impossible to condone. I felt though that I had taken a glimpse at her soul, and it didn't feel to me as if she had that in her. I did recognise that I was placing myself into a dangerous position with her. Having no transport, my only recourse was to use one of the army's covert Q cars. But it was difficult to get a work ticket signed without an operational reason, so Sinead drove us everywhere. It would be a simple matter for her to arrange for my ambush. The arrogance of youth though prevailed to make me feel invulnerable. I believed that whatever situation arose, I would be able to deal with it and I was determined to carry on, but to take great care and do my best to find out if Sinead was the monster that some people suspected her to be.

Sinead worked the night shift at Tyrone County Hospital about half a mile from Omagh's centre. We were only able to meet about twice a week, which for me was a good thing. At times of high terrorist activity I found it impossible to find time for anything, other than work, and I had a couple of other interesting brands in the fire.

In late May I had recruited a contact that lived in Dungannon, a few miles to the east of Omagh, although his work brought him into the town of Omagh. He was a republican who seemed willing to talk in general terms about Irish politics. I had lied to him by saying that I belonged to an army public relations team based at Lisanelly, and promised to get the use of a chopper for some filming that he was involved with. We met in May and three times in early June, ostensibly to discuss the best way to utilise this chopper in the limited time I had access to it.

At this time, many of the terrorist attacks in the Omagh area were being made by the grandly titled; Mid Ulster Brigade of the Provisional IRA, a scattering of Active Service Units including a group of Dungannon based volunteers supported by the local republican movement. Although Dungannon was out of our area and a different intelligence team's responsibility, I was very interested in him because he lived amongst the people who were travelling into our area to make attacks. After each meeting a contact report was completed in great detail. Captain Mike Mullen who was the Military Intelligence Officer for "M" Police Division took a particular interest. Each contact report was passed on to brigade intelligence who decided quite early on that this contact was potentially high grade, and he was given the codename of Devil Dog or DD.

As time passed the information that I was getting from this contact started to become more interesting, but never detailed. For instance he said that Lisanelly was to be attacked with mortars, and talked of possible bomb attacks on the camp. He would never detail when an attack was to take place or by whom, or even state definitely that it would happen. A mortar attack on the camp at that time didn't seem at all likely because the local IRA were felt to have neither the organisation nor equipment for such an attack. He also talked about IRA training regimes in Mountjoy Prison, and many other things. In short there was a great deal of information, which although interesting, was not operationally useful. Much of our conversation was hypothetical. Little of what was said was open and direct. Things would be alluded to rather than stated. It was as if he was simply proving his credentials in preparation for something of significance.

I remember on one occasion when he was speaking hypothetically, he said, "What if you were with army intelligence, Dave, and I was the Intelligence officer for the Mid Ulster Brigade, and us here talking like this, now wouldn't that be a thing?"
He then fell silent and watched me intently for a reaction. His normal affable and relaxed expression had disappeared and was replaced by a hard searching stare. I didn't understand what the IRA felt they were getting from these contacts, but I was sure in my own mind that they had full knowledge of them. I never doubted that he was being debriefed as thoroughly as I was at the end of these meetings. I decided that I must try to rethink my security when I met with him. The moment passed

but left a distinctly uneasy feeling. I travelled alone to the meetings, often on foot and the number of alternative routes to our meeting place, were very limited. There was no doubt that I was vulnerable to ambush, so I started to be a little more careful with him after that. Nevertheless the meetings continued.

He made an open invitation for me to visit his family home in Dungannon, saying that there were some people who I would be interested to meet. I laughed at this suggestion saying that I preferred to leave my bollocks in their present location and that a couple of bullets in the back of my head weren't high on my wish list either. He assured me on his word of honour that I would be safe and that I would find the experience worth my while. I was tempted to believe him, so later when I was making out my contact report I mentioned the offer to Mike Mullen, who reacted favourably. "We will try to set up some protective cover with 4 Field Troop," he said. The idea was that during the time that I was to be in DDs house, the MRF would mount a surveillance operation, possibly by acting as if they were working on overhead cables or they might dig a hole in the road nearby, disguised as workmen in order to be close to the house where the meeting was to tack place, just in case anything went wrong. This sort of operation was well within the remit of MRF activities.

We calculated that there were three possible

reasons for this invitation, the first being for the IRA to try to recruit me. The second possibility was that they wanted to forge some tenuous link with the army, for some reason of their own and thirdly, it might be an attempt to set up either me or the MRF. In retrospect the last of these options seemed unlikely as they would be sacrificing DD by following that course of action. In any event planning for this operation went ahead to an advanced stage until eventually someone higher up the military chain decided that it was all too risky and called the operation off. I'm not sure whether it was a concern for my welfare or that of the MRF lads that caused the change of heart. They would have been open to ambush in a bad area if it all turned out to be a trap. In truth I was beginning to get nervous myself about the whole idea but wasn't prepared to pull out and lose face. I felt like another David just about to take on Goliath, without any stones for his sling. Secretly I was glad when they called it off; it crossed my mind that both DD and I were playing an increasingly dangerous game. But after it was called off, I started to feel desperately that we had missed an important opportunity.

  She looked tired when I met her that night. Sinead's shifts at the hospital took up most of her evenings and the nights that she wasn't working were often taken up by impromptu visits from Special Branch who were still trying to nail an involvement in the pilot killings at her door. Although I was aware of these visits, we never discussed them. We sat talking quietly in her car as the thought crossed my mind that I admired her courage. Seven stone of pure guts and startling beauty. I had never met anyone like her before. I hadn't noticed that she had gone quiet. "What are you thinking about," she said.

"Nothing, just thinking what a strange couple we are."

"Couple?" she enquired, giving me a disbelieving look which she softened with a smile.

"Perhaps too strong a term," I admitted.

"David, there's something that I need to get off my chest". Other people called me Dave, she always called me David. "You know I have a son. You need to understand that if our being together should threaten him in any way, I will give you up."

"How do you mean?" I asked, looking for clarification.

"My son's safety comes first. I wouldn't want to, but if he was threatened, I would give you to them."

"Food for thought there," I replied.

The next day was the 19th of June 1973. I awoke to feel the warmth of the sun on my face and decided that it was a good day to go for breakfast in the cookhouse. The smell of burning toast and grease met me as I entered. Not for the first time I thought, I really must do something about my diet which consisted of fried food and snacks. During breakfast

I analysed what Sinead had said to me the night before. I decided that our little heart to heart must have been motivated by something. Maybe she was under some kind of pressure. I felt that there must be a reason why she needed to discuss her concerns with me last night. Having given much thought to the killing of the five soldiers, and consideration to some special secret knowledge that I had about her movements on the night of the killing, I knew she was not involved at all. Special Branch was like rabid dogs with her and once they thought they could link her they wouldn't let it go. Approving of these killings, and actually committing them, was not the same thing and she had proven to my complete satisfaction that she was somewhere else. All British soldiers were her sworn enemies; nevertheless there was something about all of it that didn't fit at all with the person that I was beginning to know. Last night she had issued a warning to me that I needed to be especially careful around her. I respected that and understood that within the parameters of our odd relationship, it was the most that I could expect.

That afternoon Lisanelly camp came under mortar attack. Six mortar shells were fired at the camp from high ground along the Gortin Road, behind the Silver Birch Hotel. No real damage was done as the IRA's new mortars fell short, landing along the camp's perimeter road. Except, that is, to the ego of one off duty soldier who was walking back to camp from the pub and was on three occasions picked up by the blast from exploding shells and thrown into the roadside hedge. Each time he extracted himself from the hedge and tried to run, another shell would explode and throw him back into the hedge. The attack was hardly noticed in RHQ, the fact that we had had weeks of prior notice of it without taking any precautions seemed to me to be more than a little bizarre. It also pissed me off greatly. What was the point of my taking big risks to get this intelligence when it wasn't being properly acted upon? I sat in on the young casualty's debrief and had great trouble keeping a straight face as he detailed the indignities of his ordeal. Thankfully he only sustained minor blast injuries and for a short while the constant ringing in his ears.

It was one week later on the 25th of June that the car with three terrorists travelling in it exploded on the Gortin road leading to the camp.

The three men from Dungannon: Carty, Loughran and Crowley were all killed. They were attempting to arm the suitcase bomb on the back seat of the car when a spark of static from the nylon shirt worn by one of the men set the device off. The destination for the bomb was thought to be Lisanelly Camp. I met up with DD a few days later and we discussed a great deal including a large bomb that had been secreted in a culvert under the Dungannon Rd. He claimed to be informing me of the bomb's whereabouts because it had failed to explode when an army patrol had been targeted with it and was now a danger to the general public. Apparently the IRA were happy to target us with their murderous devices but when that went wrong, we were expected to clean up their dangerous mess for them. No mention was made of the three dead men, or of the attack that had gone wrong; even though I knew that he lived very close to one of the dead men and would have known them all. If, as I believed, he was their intelligence officer, he would have been part of the planning for the whole disastrous operation. I thanked him for the information about the bomb and at lunch time we both made our excuses and went our separate ways. It was at this point that my suspicions that I was being used by the Mid Ulster Brigade as a tenuous link with the army became strongly reinforced. I just couldn't work out what was in it for them!

The bodies of the three terrorists who had blown themselves up on the Gortin Road were to be released from the morgue that afternoon and I was tasked by Mike Mullen to get photographs of the party who were expected to take their coffins back to Dungannon.

The morgue at Omagh was situated at the back of the hospital in an out building. There were double doors leading from an open yard into the single story building that was used as a morgue. On the opposite side of the yard about twenty yards distant, there was a small red brick building, and this was to be my observation post. Having been driven to my hide in an ambulance by an off duty UDR soldier, I entered the brick built store room taking great care not to be seen. Once inside the door was locked by the driver and he drove off leaving me wondering what another fine mess I'd got myself into! The building was about 12ft square and the door had ventilation gaps of about five inches at both its top and bottom. The room wasn't lit but the gaps let in enough light for me to see by. All that I could distinguish in the room were lots of crates containing empty bottles. If I climbed on one of these crates I found that I was able to see through the gap at the top of the door to the yard beyond. Whilst on the crate every movement that I made was accompanied by the rattling of bottles and scraping noises. I decided that this hide was impractical and that I needed to find somewhere else to fulfil my assignment. But as I had been locked in and was unable to escape from the place, I resigned myself to my situation and quietly moved things around in order to make the best of it.

After about an hour in my observation post, shuffling around uncomfortably on my crate, the coffin party arrived. There were about twelve men, dressed respectfully in suits and they proceeded straight in to the building opposite, not allowing me the chance to take the photographs that I needed to fulfil my mission. But after about ten minutes most of them came back out and stood around talking and smoking in the space between my hideaway and the double doors of the Morgue. It was like a who's who of the IRA. I recognised many of them from photographs, and one who had been with me just two hours before, it was Devil Dog.

Some of the party came across and leaned against the building where I hid. I could smell their cigarette smoke and clearly hear them talking. The shutter on my SLR camera seemed very loud in the confined space of the store room and I was intensely aware of the closeness of those smoking outside. I started to wonder what their reaction would be if they heard my shutter and decided to look through the gaps in the door. I understood perfectly well the consequences if I was discovered. After about fifteen minutes of hardly breathing, whatever the logjam had been to the proceedings in the morgue, it was cleared and the three coffins were removed to the waiting vehicles. When they had all left for the wake it wasn't too long before I was released from my incarceration, and taken back round to the hospital car park by the ambulance. My relationship with Devil Dog was to continue for nearly a year until I left Ireland.

A week later, the 500 lb of explosives that made up

the bomb that I had been informed about by DD was
removed from its resting place in the culvert under
the Dungannon Road and transported by means of a
battered old covert Transit van and under the cover
of darkness it was replanted. Its new home was
under a bridge at an illegal border crossing. The
crossing had been a thorn in our side for some time
and numerous attempts had been made by the army
to block it off, even using bulldozers to destroy the
road on the northern side. But within days a crowd
of republicans and locals would turn up to
reconstitute the crossing. The bridge itself spanned
the border with the Republic and so was arguably
partly in the Republic, so someone had the bright
idea of reusing the device in order to permanently
take out the bridge that was being used as a border
crossing point. At first light we re-found the device
which I thought of as a gift to me from the IRA in its
new location and called the ATO who used a "none
too controlled explosion" in order to destroy the
bomb and in doing so, blew the offending bridge to
kingdom come, therefore denying its use for
importing weapons and explosives to the North.

I met up with Sinead as often as I was able to;
sometimes she was in the company of a girl called
Angy or Big Angy. She wasn't really that big; I
supposed it was the case of comparing her against
Sinead. I was never sure what these two were up to
but felt strongly that Sinead supplied the cunning,

while Big Angy supplied the muscle, we still strongly suspected that this dubious partnership were intelligence gathering for the Provisionals.

One night when the three of us were standing at the bar of a pub on Market Street in Omagh a large local youth elbowed my drink over. Turning around I noted the sharp look and muttered command from Angy to the youth who had an immediate change of attitude and offered to buy me a replacement drink, which I accepted. I had noticed this character in the background before. He would often show up where we were, and kept distant tabs on us. On one occasion when he was watching me from the opposite end of the bar in a pub on Bridge Street in Omagh; a UDR soldier who I knew well walked in and I saw a flash of recognition between them and a stiffening of defensive body language. The soldier whose name was Carl came over and stood with me at the bar, he knew instantly who I was talking about when I asked. "Who is he?"

I wasn't surprised to hear that according to Carl, he was a provisional IRA man from Tyrone, east of Omagh. Although the locals sometimes displayed a rather bigoted view of some of their neighbours, you needed to listen to what they had to say. They knew most of the answers, if only you where clever enough to filter out the crap and see what was left.

Carl asked how long he'd been in the pub, which was

a regular squaddie haunt. I just answered that I didn't know and lied that I had never seen him before. The UDR were heroes, but there was always a chance that some of their chatter might get through to Prod paramilitaries, and I didn't fancy lugging the carcass of the man, who I thought of as Sinead's minder, into a body bag in the next couple of days. It was a good thing to be aware of all the potential threats that you perceived around you, but any suspicions that you held were best kept to yourself and only acted upon when there was something to be gained by it.

Above: The bomb squad deploying wheelbarrow to get a close look at a suspected car bomb, Wheelbarrow, the bomb disposal robot saved a lot of lives right from its introduction in 1972.

Below Left: Ron on the morning of the multiple letter bombing. The bombs were made by hollowing out copies of Readers Digest and filling the void with plastic explosives and a commercial detonator. The device was detonated when the package was opened, by a circuit being completed when the book was being removed from the packaging. Ron is seen in the photograph, setting up a controlled explosion, in order to disarm the device.

Below Right: A bomb consisting of 1 lb of Semtex plastic explosive, with a kitchen timer, disguised in a transistor radio case. The device was dismantled by ATO in early 1974.

Bottom Left & Right: Ron on the morning of the multiple letter bombing. The bombs were made by hollowing out copies of Readers Digest and filling the void with plastic explosives and a commercial detonator. The device was detonated when the package was opened, by a circuit being completed when the book was being removed from the packaging. Ron is seen in the photograph, setting up a controlled explosion, in order to disarm the device.

1st IRA VCP

In '73 the IRA started throwing up Vehicle Check Points or VCPs in country areas in order, in their own words, 'to catch out Army snoopers and touts and to stamp their authority on an area.' They were also very keen to get hold of members of the Ulster Defence Regiment in order to murder them. South Tyron, Fermanagh and Armagh were their favourite areas. The VCPs where often well thought out with anything up to ten or twelve men involved in each. They would have one or two men acting as long-stop; fifty or so yards either side of a knife edge which was manned by more armed men. They then stopped traffic and questioned the car's occupants. The normal outcome of the stop was that the terrified driver would be allowed to continue his journey, but not always! It was normal for military personnel unlucky enough to get caught in this way to be dragged to the side of the road and executed. Or be taken away and tortured for information before being disposed of.

I ran into my first IRA VCP in mid '73. I was

travelling as a passenger in Sinead's Mini Clubman
at about 9 pm on a dark weekday evening. By this
stage in the conflict the IRA had become very
proficient at mounting Vehicle Check Points. They
had learned a lot from watching the army. They
would set up their VCP and stop a few vehicles and
then move to a new location to repeat the process.
After two or three moves they would pack up before
the army heard about their activities and responded.
Their checkpoints were normally set up in rural
areas, particularly those areas that the IRA already
dominated. They were manned by a mixture of
irregulars and local men under the command of a
regular volunteer. Their main force was at the
stopping point, but they usually kept a man armed
with a sub machine gun or automatic rifle at about
fifty or so yards distance either side of the stopping
point to act as a long stop. His job was to prevent
any attempt at escape by vehicles approaching or
leaving the trap. The check point would stamp the
IRA's authority on these country areas as well as
filtering out any covert army or UDR movement, in
what they thought of as their areas. Sinead and her
friend Angy both had strong family links with this
part of county Tyrone, which was currently the
centre for this type of activity.

  We were travelling along a narrow country road
between Carickmore and Omagh when things
started to go wrong. I had no immediate feeling of

alarm when I sighted the lights of the VCP at a bend in the road a few hundred yards ahead; it was obviously an Army or UDR Vehicle Checkpoint, but as we got closer I could see that the soldiers all wore masks and irregular non-standard camouflage clothing. A nauseous feeling took over my whole person as I scrambled for the browning pistol in my hip holster. I had no idea what I would do with it considering that there where at least twelve armed terrorists about to confront me, so I laid it on my lap, covering it with my jacket. I felt something half way between terror and elation and as we passed the long stop I noted that the weapon that he was carrying was an American Armalite rifle. We obeyed his slow down signal and stopped behind another stationary car.

My mind was racing; there was no doubt about the outcome if they captured me. In the whole of the campaign to date, I knew of no security force member who was ever released alive after capture. My thoughts were of torture and death. It was an easy decision to make, I would go down fighting. Sinead was driving the car, so making a run for it wasn't within my control, and would anyway have meant certain death for both myself in the back of the car and the two young women in the front. There was sure to be a long stop further down the road to riddle us with bullets as we tried to pass. To make things worse both of my companions in the vehicle were suspected of having strong links with the Provo's. I half expected them to just say, "Here he is, take him," but nothing was said. I felt as if my body was a coiled spring ready to explode into action but at the same time hoping beyond hope that I wouldn't need to. The weight of my concealed weapon laid across my legs was reassuring. It was at times like this that one magazine with only nine rounds of ammunition felt totally inadequate.

I don't know whether the girls felt that they might not fare well in a shoot-out, or whether it was their humanity that interceded on my behalf, or in Sinead's case I knew that she was starting to have feelings for me. Whatever the reason, they said nothing.

A group of men with weapons were milling around the car that had been stopped in front of us. A number of torches emitted shafts of light around the scene and animated voices filled the void of the night. The index finger of my right was balanced against the trigger of the pistol, which was now directed at the car door panel and aiming straight at the genitals of the masked man who was approaching my side of the Mini Clubman. I remember thinking that this was just a teenager, and by the looks of him he was no more than sixteen or seventeen years old. He was of wiry build, with long fair hair and carrying an old assault rifle. This was the moment of truth. Any aggressive movement from him and I would shoot him through the flimsy door panel and exit the car and break for cover.

The only trouble with this course of action was that we where now within feet of the main group of terrorists, but it would be the only option that I had, and then again, maybe the element of surprise would help me to attain the sparse tree cover at the road side. He bent to look at me in the back of the car and seemed to stare at me for ages before he took a closer look at the girls. He appeared to recognise Sinead straight away and looked a little uncomfortable. Angy, who was sitting in front of me in the front passenger seat and nearest to the approaching man leaned her face towards the open window of the car and snarled, "Fucking idiot," at him.

During all this time Sinead's face was a mask of cool determination. She glanced around at me in the back, and I detected a flicker of concern and reassurance. The gun man just straightened up, and turning away, walked back to the group. He spoke to a lean man in his early twenties who had a mask covering the lower half of his face. The man glanced round at us, mumbled something that I didn't quite catch and the boy turned and casually waved us through. For my part I can admit to being terrified but determined not to be taken alive. It was to be 37 years before Sinead and I ever spoke about that incident and over those long years it had left a great many unanswered questions in my mind.

After that night I can honestly say that I know the true meaning of desperation. In retrospect I believe that those few minutes defined who I would be for the rest of my life. It's the most difficult thing to make the decision that I might have had to make that night, but not nearly so hard as to go back to being the person that you were before it. I don't think I ever found my way back.

Three of the young men who made up that Vehicle Check Point including the one who waved us through were ambushed and killed by the SAS a few years later, only half a mile away from the spot where we were stopped.

I never discussed my activities with Sinead and she never spoke about whatever she got up to. Once again it was to be long after the end of the IRA campaign before I got any idea what her true involvement was and everything that I did find out came from other sources.

On July 10th a mobile patrol from 1RTR came under attack when targeted by a large land mine. The IRA firing point 200 yards away in the Republic was heavily engaged by members of the patrol after they managed to extricate themselves from their two bomb blasted vehicles. Within an hour I had reached the scene of the attack to find most of C Sqn's

Assault troop busy clearing up the bits of wreckage from the patrol's badly damaged vehicles and covering the nearby border with arcs of fire, in case of further attacks. Amongst them was my old mate Ron Woods. Ron was now the troop sergeant with Assault troop, but many years before we were both in another world, fighting a different enemy. As I approached I saw that one of the soldiers had set up a Benghazi cooker at the side of the road and was making a brew. The troop's present role was as infantry support for our mobile patrols.

I remember thinking. "You can take the boy out of the tank but you can't take the tank out of the boy." There was always something quite endearing about the way the 'Tanky' always found a way to improve even the worst location that he found himself in. Ron directed the volunteer chef to find a cup for me,

"Oh! And make it NATO standard," he directed. (NATO standard tea was squady speak for milk and two sugars).

We found a couple of old fertiliser bags that the Provos had hung on fence posts to act as aiming markers for their remotely detonated culvert mine, and used them to sit on for half an hour, reminiscing about the old days back in Aden where we had first met.

Aden, South Arabia

(Republic of Yemen) 130 years as part of the British Empire

The New Labour Government disbanded the Territorial Army, brought in swingeing cuts to the military budget and gave in to the rebels and Arab Nationalists in South Arabia and the Yemen. After wasting the lives of hundreds of young soldiers we started a bloody withdrawal. Which marked the end of empire? At the same time as this foolish short sighted policy was being enacted, the civil war that was raging in the Yemen was further enflamed by the British Government sending a Squadron of SAS to fight for the royalist cause. The 100 or so soldiers of the SAS, who were required to temporarily leave the British Army, made an enormous difference, but it wasn't enough. Their secret war trailed on until the royalist cause seemed hopeless, then they rejoined the British Army. The days of benign governance had ended; it didn't fit in with the new Arab nationalism which was sweeping across the Middle East.

It had all started years before during the Suez Crisis. Thanks to an intervention by our American allies, the British and French lost control of the Canal Zone and ended up leaving behind hundreds of tonnes of arms, ammunition and explosives during their hasty withdrawal. Gamil Abdul Nasser (Egyptian President) re- exported much of this state of the art weaponry to the Yemen and South Arabia to fuel the civil war in the Yemen and the revolt against the British in the south. The long term effect of this was that most of the Arab world exchanged its fatherly shackles for brutal murderous dictatorships for the next fifty years, and are only now shedding these chains.

Many of these countries which had their own traditional kind of leadership were quickly forced to revolutionary styles of governance instead of evolving more free democratic systems, with acceptable traditional links. Of course, as with most revolutionary systems they very quickly and predictably became brutal dictatorships and moved swiftly to the left or right politically. Our Cold War enemies took full advantage, filling the void both militarily and ideologically. Within two years the Labour government found that they had to reinstate the Territorial Army because it became obvious, even to them, that it constituted a major part of the country's military strength. After their foolish and expensive, politically motivated piece of nonsense, they left the armed forces alone for a while and concentrated on wrecking the economy. In some ways the US's unhelpful intervention at the time of the Suez Crisis was beneficial to us. For one thing we would almost certainly have got embroiled in the Vietnam War was it not for the fact that nationally, we were still pissed off with the yanks over Suez.

At the same time that all this was happening, a very young looking 20 year old soldier who had just finished his basic training was setting foot on the runway at RAF Khormaksar in South Arabia. It was two o'clock in the morning on the 20th of November 1965. The temperature was hovering around 85F and the ripe pungent smell of rotting vegetation filled his nostrils. There was a terminal building of sorts, but it was presently out of use because of a grenade attack that had taken place the previous day. It must have been one hell of a grenade, judging by the destruction which was visible through the open doors. A soldier with a strong Irish accent approached me and asked if I was heading for Falaise Camp. He gave me a pitying look when I informed him that I didn't know. "Are you 1 RTR?" he demanded, to which I nodded confirmation. "Jump in that," he said, indicating with a pointed finger at a tatty old green single decked bus, which had a ragged hole in the bodywork on the front, near side. I did as directed. "What happened to the bus," I asked the sullen looking man next to me. "How the fuck would I know" he snarled at me. "It was hit last week by a rocket while doing this trip," said one of the Enniskillen Dragoon Guards who was doing escort duty. He was seated at the front of the bus behind the driver and cradling his sub machine gun in his arms. "That was the third time they've hit the bus in the last two months," he added. "Fucking bastards," muttered my companion before glancing out of the window at the hail of fire flies that were hissing past us in the night. "They look just like fucking tracer," he said. The thought had already crossed my mind but in order not to sound a wimp I had kept it to myself.

Little Aden, where the camp was situated, was on the opposite side of a huge bay from the rest of the coastal townships that made up Aden. The British had built an enormous causeway across the bay in a large arc, making the journey of about twenty five miles considerably shorter. The causeway had large security checkpoints at either end. Checkpoint Charley was on the Aden end of the causeway and Checkpoint Delta was at the Little Aden end. Our bus had rattled its way through the darkened townships of this desert domain until we were stopped at the brightly lit checkpoint Charley. It didn't take long for the queue of cars and brightly painted trucks that were often used to transport the local people around the protectorate to be dealt with and we were once again on our way. By this time I had discovered that my grumpy friend was a member of my regiment and that furthermore we were to be in the same troop. His name was Ron Woods and we were destined to become lifelong friends.

The whole of the southern part of Arabia was at this time made up of dozens of small Sheikhdoms and emirates ruled by traditional leaders. The western side of this area was linked in federation and protected by the British. This had the effect of controlling some of the more extreme actions of their feudal leaders, but recognizing and respecting their Islamic culture whilst giving security to the region. Some of the eastern emirates were also linked together in federation, friendly to Britain and to a degree supported militarily by us. The affect of South Arabia on a young soldier like me was to think that I had stepped back a thousand years into a mystical land, where trade was still carried out in great wooden sailing ships and apart from the coastal strip, the inhabitants walked about their towns armed to the teeth; a place of magic and wonderment. Camel trains with hundreds of people and animals would appear out of the desert as if from nowhere at some ungodly hour of the night.
  At first the whole place made your senses tingle but your feelings started to change with recognition of the communist inspired insurgency that we found ourselves combating. When I arrived there, South Arabia's recent history was one of warfare and

revolt. Our force of arms had just defeated a major revolt in the fertile mountainous Radfan region, and was now, along with federal forces combating a better armed and more insidious kind of ideological war throughout the federation.

What did I know of war or the aspirations of nations? I had just finished basic training at Catterick in north Yorkshire, where they had taught me how to kill without thinking about my enemy as anything but targets, and was now keen to put those skills to the test. The naive over simplifications of youth, for me, as for all of us, left my conscience clear.

On arrival at the camp we were shown to a hut where I spent the rest of the night sitting, smoking cigarettes and drinking coffee and listening to the noises made by the air conditioners until morning. At daybreak I followed everyone through the searing heat of the new day to the cookhouse where breakfast was being served. The cereal that I chose appeared to have lots of small insects swimming around it, and when I complained I was told that was normal. "Anyway the weevils are extra meat ration, lad," muttered the cook sergeant with a sneer on his face. Invariably all the food that we ate for the next year was of a similar disgusting standard. I recognize that cooking for soldiers was a thankless job but these guys gave a whole new meaning to the words culinary delight. Thank god for the army's compo rations, at least they were nutritious and un-recycled.

After breakfast I discovered that my regiment had not yet arrived from the UK, and that I would be spending a week with the 5th Enniskillen Dragoon Guards, or as they were more generally known, the 5th Skins. Little did I know that the Enniskillen would play a big part in my future.

Mostly recruited in Northern Ireland the 5th Skins were an armoured cavalry regiment with a long and glorious tradition dating back before the Napoleonic Wars. One of the first things that I noticed about them was their propensity to good natured religious conflict. This just occasionally seemed to become more serious. I remember asking one of them what a Feenian bastard was, having heard the term a number of times. I was most surprised to discover from his answer that I was one! All in all though, they were an excellent Unit.

An advance party of 1RTR had started to arrive in station about a week earlier, amongst whom was an old Polish soldier who had got stranded in the regiment at the end of WW2. He was now running C Sqn stores and had come into possession of a scabby, flee bitten old dog that had been passed over to him by the outgoing unit. The dog, recognizing a meal ticket, followed him everywhere and was quite defensive of his newly found master. To the point, in fact, that he was likely to take a lump out of the leg of anyone who went near him. The morning after my arrival in Falaise I was told to go to the Polish corporal's stores and draw out a mattress and some blankets. All the squadrons' stores and equipment were kept in a single story building, which was close to the accommodation lines. As I arrived there I was confronted by the sight of the old polish corporal knocking the hell out of a Fifth Skin. One great big hairy Scouser grabbed the Pole, lifted his feet of the ground, and restrained him from further assaulting the unhappy Irish man. The Pole, who's English was in fact excellent, was so incensed by an attack on his dog that he reverted to a kind of pigeon English. "Why for you kick my dog and call him fuck off," the Pole demanded.

For most of the time that I spent in South Arabia I felt completely knackered. It wasn't just the challenge posed by the extreme desert conditions but also our work cycle that left little time for anything but sleep, and there was never enough of that. Every third night was spent on either guard duty or Internal Security mobile patrol in Aden. As a regiment we had the dual roles of contributing fully towards the protectorate's internal security by means of foot patrols, as well as the aforementioned mobile patrols, and maintaining the only British heavy armoured presence in the region. Our effort leaned mainly towards the heavy armoured recognisance role, but we did also have two sabre squadrons one of which was often on board the Royal Navy's only LST (Landing Ship Tank). HMS Striker was left over from World War 2 and was due to be replaced by HMS Fearless, Britain's new, and state of the art commando carrier. When it was our squadron's turn for this duty, we sailed up and down the Persian Gulf to project force. Our 12 Tanks in a rusty old American built tub was supposed to impress our neighbours about the UKs commitment to the region.

Our Internal Security patrols mostly took place in Aden and Shake Othman, and normally constituted a couple of Land Rovers that had a driver and commander in the front, and a gunner and radio operator in the back of the open vehicle. This configuration was good in that it gave the gunner all round vision but proved bad in that the open vehicle was an excellent receptacle for dissident hand grenades. Mustafa Go and friends deposited their newly acquired British Mills 36 grenades into the backs of our Land Rovers as they negotiated the narrow streets of Aden and Sheikh Othman on a nightly basis.

The answer, according to the army, was not to buy new and special vehicles! No, the answer was to designate the wireless operator as a grenade finder.

111

When one of these attacks occurred, the gunner focused on returning fire and the radio operator scrambled around on his hands and knees trying to find, and eject the miscreant missile, preferably before it went off. The driver would then put his foot to the floor in order to put some distance between the soon to explode grenade and his vehicle. Night after bloody night this bizarre scenario took place. One radio operator belonging to an infantry unit had to do this at the same place, two nights in a row, and that without recognition of any kind. After a while we learnt to leave our vehicles empty of all except necessary equipment in order to speed up the radio operators search.

The grenades had either seven or four second fuses in them, which left very little time from them leaving the grenadiers hand to exploding. If you take two seconds off that for it to travel through the air that leaves only two very short seconds for the radio operator to find and eject it from the vehicle, and for the vehicle to travel far enough to be out of the grenade's killing range. It was all like some kind of a sick video game, and not at all good for the crew's blood pressure. One major setback to this tactic of scooping the grenade up and dropping it out of the back of the Land Rover was that if the attack was on the first vehicle, the second or subsequent vehicle might easily find itself over the exploding Mills grenade.

One of the tactics that the army employed to combat these grenade attacks was to send out groups of undercover soldiers dressed as Arabs and armed to the teeth. They would move undetected through the streets of Sheikh Othman and lay in ambush for dissidents near to their favourite grenade throwing spots.

A bright lad in Intelligence thought up another scheme, and they fed a box of mills grenades to the dissidents that were fitted with instant fuses. Instead of exploding after four or seven seconds, they went off instantly in the terrorist's hand. After a few of these unfortunate incidents the number of grenade attacks fell off sharply for a while.

Twice during my one year tour I did long range desert patrols. We took with us a medic who would treat people in the villages that we visited. None of the local inhabitants had ever taken antibiotics so the drugs often performed miraculous cures on them. One problem though was that it was deemed, discourteous in Bedouin society, to give to one member of the family without also giving to the others. The way around this was to give the drug to the sick person and everyone else got placebos. We needed to be extremely careful in the villages, there were as few as two or three of us on some occasions with a great many armed and possibly dissident tribesmen around. The Bedu though, exercised strict rules of etiquette, killing the Hakeem 'Doctor' during his visit would have been frowned upon in tribal society. South Arabia, we were told had upwards of 70,000 dissident tribesmen and not only them but everyone else too was armed to the teeth. They looked incredible in their traditional dress with bandoleers of ammunition draped around their torsos whilst carrying their ornate rifles and the curved jambiya dagger at their waist.

We dished out medicine during the day and then found ourselves under attack at night and the next day we did the same thing over again. It was quite possible, in fact likely, that the people who we were medicating during the day where involved in the night time attacks. Thankfully they were lousy shots and often fired rockets at us from two or three times their maximum range. They did do better with their new British anti tank Mk 7 land mines, courtesy of Abdul Nasser,
I can remember one going off under a Saracen armoured personnel carrier that was just in front of me. One of its wheels and the suspension shot about 150 feet up into the air, and rained down onto the other vehicles in the convoy. One of our officers, Captain Robinson Fox was unlucky enough to ride over a MK 7 mine in a Land Rover. He was killed instantly while his driver was very seriously injured. At night we would form a defensive leaguer and

'stand too', in anticipation of an attack. At first light, our defensive posture was also increased. The patrols lasted anything up to a month or six weeks in duration, and caused a lot of health problems amongst the lads. But like the heroes they were, they just grumbled and carried on.

The tour felt never ending. Most of the lads kept a 'Days to Do' chart in their lockers. In my case it started off with 365 small squares on a sheet of paper and as the time passed the boxes were ticked off. At about the tour's half way point, I was given R and R leave (rest and recuperation) in Mombasa. Kenya was lush and green compared with Arabia and the three weeks that I spent there were very relaxing. It was a weird sensation and new experience, some of the flying insects appeared to be the size of house bricks, and all the various forms of insects bit, but what a place.

On arrival at the army's Silver Sands Leave Centre we were all shown to our accommodation in very comfortable chalet type buildings. There we found a mass of paperwork detailing the dos and don'ts. Highest on the list of don'ts was a warning not to contract STDs from the pretty girls that could be met in the many bars. It was classed as a self inflicted injure and chargeable under military law. Mombasa was very lush and tropical compared with Aden's dry hot climate. After discovering the town and its constant rhythmic pulse of drum beats, I headed to the local beach to watch the hundreds of nubile, semi naked women, and drool as they frolicked in the surf. This was a different world and it all belonged to me for the next three weeks.

Later in the day I decided to explore the area. There were several large expensive looking hotels along the coast, the nearest of these being the Nialy Beach hotel. I had never seen such luxury. In 1965 only well- off people went to Africa for their holidays, and this was a glimpse of how the other half lived. On the beach in front of the hotel I met a couple of gorgeous looking German girls. They were on holiday before starting their teaching careers. Neither of them spoke any English, and I spoke no German, so communication was difficult for me but our meeting up opened some adventurous possibilities for them, and maybe for me! We went everywhere that would have been a problem for two women without an able bodied chaperon. Working on the theory that if I was able to peel one of them off, I might get some safe sex, I stayed on my best behaviour. For the remaining two weeks of their holiday, we were inseparable, and I never managed to get my evil way, but we all had a great time.

They never knew that I was a soldier and that at the end of my holiday I would have to go back to a war zone; it just didn't seem appropriate to tell them.

When they eventually went back home to Germany I still had six days left and very little money, so just spent my time chilling out. My R and R was a great success, it left me with some priceless memories and a colossal hard on.

I flew back to Aden with a feeling of well being that quickly evaporated in the Arabian heat. The fighting in and around Aden was increasing and more attacks against security forces were occurring every day.

One evening I found myself in Khormaksar, I had been told that there was a Chinese tailor there who would hand cut a suit for me for 30 quid. His shop was in the middle of a small parade in a military area. It was dusk, I had been measured for my suit and was making my way back to where I was to meet my lift, when five or six three ton army trucks pulled up. Within a minute or two the whole area was swarming with soldiers. A company of the now defunct Somerset and Cornwall Light Infantry were loading up ready to go back up country. These weren't parade ground soldiers; they were hard fighting men on their way back to operations. Their kit was worn threadbare and they were loaded down with weapons and extra ammunition as they climbed abroad the waiting wagons. It didn't matter to them that our government was already in the process of giving in to the enemy. They were off to

117

do what they did best, fight. I thought to myself. "These men are my brothers."

As well has having our Internal Security duties to perform, we also had to maintain our two Squadrons of 15 + Centurion Tanks, and that meant endlessly practicing our gunnery and radio skills. Because of the demands of the Internal Security situation, it was difficult to find time for exercises, but early in the tour 'A' Squadron went up country in an area called The Jabal Khariz. It was our first opportunity to work together as a tank crew. Yorky, who was a veteran of the regiment's time in Korea, was our commander, (Ginger) Mainard who was tall with a shock of red hair our driver, (Pancho) Rodriguez, the youngest and newest member of the crew our radio operator, and I was gunner. Although I didn't at that time to have Gunnery as a trade, I was the experienced tank gunner from my time in the 40th 41st Royal Tank Regiment, Territorial Army.

The exercise was going well when a radio message came through directing us to park up for a couple of hours and feed ourselves. 2 Troop, of which I was a member, chose a waddy at the side of a Jebel with a good view of the desert to the south of us. When we dismounted from our tanks, to set up our Benghazi, Pancho brought to our attention some very unusual looking track marks in the sand. There were various views about which vehicle made track marks like this. Someone suggested that it might be from one of our half tracks? But no, we agreed that they were too wide for that, then Pancho had us all laughing when he vehemently stated that he knew what they were. He claimed to have seen those tracks on a tank in the Bovington Tank Museum back in the UK.

"They are Russian T 34 tracks," he said with conviction.
Ginger replied, "Shut the fuck up, Pancho, and put that kettle on."
When the brew arrived we sat watching the distant tank movements out in the desert. We were all having a break but at least one troop was still manoeuvring. Our troop had neither live nor blank ammunition on board for our 105mm gun which was the tank's main armament; we only had our small arms ammo. But those buggers out there seemed to be popping away with main armament blanks at each other. "How far away do you think they are?" said Ginger to Yorky. "Five or six miles I should think," he replied, and after some thought added. "It's difficult to tell in the desert."
   "They are probably Panchos T34s," someone remarked, and we all started laughing.
   Right about then a small group of tribesmen arrived astride their camels and we went through all the greeting formalities. They looked friendly enough but you never could tell. Yorky detailed

Pancho into the turret of one of the tanks with his SMGT and told the Arabs NOT to unsling their weapons. They were cool with that, but did we have cigarettes?

I had been admiring an ancient Martini Henry rifle which one of them was carrying, so I offered to buy it from him. Eventually we agreed a price which included a pack of cigarettes and a few Dinars. When the negotiations were complete the tribesmen moved on and the desert to the south was empty once more. We carried on with the exercise.

Two days later after we had arrived back in Aden, we heard on the radio that there were reports of a tank battle having spilled over the border from the Yemen into the Jabal Khariz area. There was no living with Pancho after that. The Yemeni rebels did own a number of old Russian T34 Tanks.

HMS Striker
HMS Striker was a Landing Ship Tank or LST that had been built along with a great many similar ships by the Americans for the 'D' Day landings. Many of these vessels never did another days work and were eventually towed off to the scrap yard. In the case of Striker though, she was assigned to the Royal Navy under the Lend Lease scheme and was still in service, chugging up and down the Persian Gulf twenty years later, by 1965 her days were

numbered.

These LSTs were designed to beach themselves in order to discharge their load of main battle tanks through great bow doors at the fore end, directly on to the shore and ready to fight. Her hold would take a Squadron of 12 Centurion tanks and one Beach Armoured Recovery Vehicle that was a specially built Centurion that had no gun turret and had a weird looking steel skirting welded and sticking up and around it in order to keep out water when doing vehicle recovery work on the beach. The Barv as it was known was a very odd looking contraption, but was invaluable for wet landings. The upper structure of Striker was used for carrying all the Squadron's necessary B vehicles, along with all the supplies that a squadron needed when on the move.

As well as the beaching method of discharging Strikers load, there was also the Rhino. The Rhino, another Lend Lease item, was basically a huge raft that was normally towed around by Striker. It was possible with care to off load up to 3 Centurions onto the Rhino at a time in open sea, then land them by beaching the Rhino. This was the theory, but when 2 troop tried it the weather took a fast turn for the worse and we came close to losing three Centurion Tanks at sea. The increasingly heavy seas meant that we were unable to either land on shore or reattach to Striker in order to evacuate our tanks from the Rhino. It had to sail around the coast and find a more sheltered bay in which we could land. What should have been a ten minute journey from ship to shore turned into a four hour cruise around the South Arabian shore line in worsening weather conditions. Half an hour into our cruise the navy discovered that one of the buoyancy tanks that made up the twenty year old raft's base had failed and was now full of water. The craft was taking on an unpleasant list to starboard and discreet enquiries were being made by the navy as to whether or not everyone was able to swim.

Our troop Sergeant, Yorky Creaser, was trying to discover what paperwork would be required if he lost his complete troop of tanks at sea. In short the whole exercise turned into a complete farce. The navy, bless them, hated having all us "PONGOS" on board. They tried to get us to stop saying sharp end, blunt end and middle bit when referring to their boat. Sorry! I mean SHIP!. It was haft, stern and mid ship, port and starboard, not left side and right side. In fact we did it even more because we knew how much it irritated them. All in all though, they were good hosts and each day after lunch we received our rum ration.

We became quite proficient at the beach landings and further up the Gulf took part in a big live fire exercise.

There is an uninhabited island off the coast belonging to our allies, the United Arab Emirates called Yas. The island consisted of two and a half miles by two miles of desert with mountains in the middle. The RAF was to bomb the mountains, while we, with a battalion of paras, were to land and take objectives along the coastal strip. The paras were dropped in by parachute at first light and within two hours, (when the temperature had risen above 160 degrees F,) the whole exercise had to be called off. Apparently the paras were dropping like flies with heat exhaustion and we fared little better in our tanks. We couldn't wait to re-board Striker and sail on to Kuwait. Eventually we arrived back in Aden after having sailed through heavy monsoon seas in our twisting and rolling flat bottomed ship and were relieved to get our size nine boots firmly back on shore. We had been away for two and a half months while the security situation in Aden had worsened. That night I revisited my, days to do chart.

Keeni Meeni
The dissidents were particularly strong in the Sheikh Othman Township which was situated a few miles to the north west of Aden itself. Sheikh Othman was a scruffy sprawling town with open sewers and tightly packed, low grade dwellings that smelled of an acrid mixture of decaying food, sewage and smelly armpits. It was also a great

Special Forces play ground. In order to cut down the number of grenade attacks on our mobile patrols, SAS and other specialist teams took to the murky back alleys almost nightly, setting ambushes for the Dizzies (Dissidents) grenade throwers and machine gunners. These operations were usually very successful, but would occasionally go wrong.

On more than one occasion this activity ended up in blue on blue gunfights. For instance there was an occasion when two heavily armed groups of Arabs met up and engaged in an extended gun battle before finding out that one of the groups was SAS and the other belonged to the Kings Own Yorkshire Light Infantry. If I remember correctly, both sides took casualties and there were red faces all round afterwards.

The Keeni Meeni, (from Swahili and meaning, like a snake) Operations were also very good for following up informant leads and either capturing or killing known terrorists.

I can remember on one occasion that our patrol was ordered to Steamer Point to pick up one man. We were to take a hooded informer from intelligence HQ to indicate for us a terrorist suspect in the back streets of S O, every part of the informant's body, even his hands were covered by the garment that the army had supplied for him. The effect was finished off with a Ku Klux Klan style pointed hood on top, complete with eye holes. He walked up to his target and pointed with an outstretched arm. What happened next was out of order. The soldier escorting him; wearing plain jungle greens which showed no indication of rank or regiment started a frenzied attack using his fists against the Arab. Within seconds the man was an unconscious ruin on the ground. To class this man as a prisoner when the attack took place is a matter of conjecture, but I would have thought his humanity alone would have qualified him for better treatment than he received. I'm ashamed to say that I said or did nothing during this incident, but I wasn't alone in that, nor did the officer supposedly in command of the patrol. In the hour or so that we stayed together as a patrol I never saw that man regain consciousness. Nor was it a good feeling driving through Sheikh Othman in our open Land Rover with the unconscious prisoner, an obvious informer and the Unknown Soldier in his unrecognisable uniform and wearing a mask. I would describe the feeling as one of vulnerability and disbelief. When I thought about it afterward, I assumed that, as we had picked the assailant and informer up at intelligence HQ, the soldier must have been Slime, (Intelligence Corps) or SAS. It proved one thing to me, and that was that no matter how good we thought we were we were by no means perfect.

On the outskirts of the town of Sheikh Othman at a

place called El Mansura there was a prison where captured dissidents were interned. On a couple of occasions Ron and I did guard duty there. We never saw what went on inside, we were only allowed in the pill boxes that Lined the prison's fortified walls. I do remember that there always seemed to be a stream of cars driving around the perimeter road blasting their horns, that and the occasional sound of gunfire and explosions from the nearby streets.

On the road in front of the prison about quarter of a mile away there was a traffic island with a heavily fortified bunker mounted in the middle of it, which was manned by soldiers 24 hours a day. Grenade Corner, as it was known, was attacked 2 or 3 times every week. Its construction was of steel plates and sandbags and the exterior of this bunker was strewn with the debris of numerous previous attacks.

Sometime towards the end of 1965 HMS Striker chugged off into the sunset to be made into razor blades and dog food cans and in its place the navy received the brand new HMS Fearless, first of the UKs Commando Carriers. What an amazing difference! From having to sleep on deck because of the cramped, smelly mess decks that Striker boasted, we were suddenly in air conditioned, almost luxurious accommodation with closed circuit TV. On top of this the food was vastly better, the Navy being the senior service, always got better food than we did and they issued butter where we received margarine. Whenever we were on board one of their ships they would feed us with proper food.

The ship was built on a totally different concept to what HMS Striker had been. The whole of Fearless's stern was open so that landing craft were able to sail inside her. As with Striker, Fearless was able to accommodate a large number of tanks and B vehicles, which by means of its state of the art landing craft; it could disembark in most weather conditions. In short she was beautiful and 'A' Squadron were to be the first troops to take her to war. The whole of the squadron was to mount a big fighting patrol along the Federations border with the Yemen. We would sail North West from Aden and make a landing when we met the unmarked Yemeni border and from there we would make an epic journey inland following the border through the desert region for hundreds of miles. For the first time ever we were to take with us our own air support in the form of a Sioux helicopter to be used for reconnaissance flights. The patrol had duel objectives; its primary objective was to check the border for incursions from the civil war that was raging in the Yemen. Its secondary one was to interdict the movement of dissidents, and their weapons into the Federation.

The Communist supported revolt against the British backed royalist forces in the Yemen had, on a number of occasions, spilled across into the empty sector of the Federation. Only a few months earlier a tank battle had been reported, which took place on Federation territory. Our patrol was made up of mainly armoured personnel carriers and armoured cars with soft skin B vehicles carrying our fuel and supplies. Everything had to go with us. There were no roads on our route, never mind filling stations, all our food, ammunition, fuel and water needed to be carried on the B vehicles.

The temperatures in the desert were blisteringly hot, if we had had the luxury of an egg we could have cooked it in a couple of minutes by just breaking it on our vehicle's metal exterior.

We kept our drinking water in canvas bags slung on the outside of our vehicles. The action of the sun and wind caused a process of evaporation that kept the water inside lovely and cool. Each crew cooked their own food on Benghazi cookers. A Benghazi (named after the town in Libya) was made by driving four tank track pins into the ground to form a stand for the cooking pot, old food tins were filled with sand and soaked in petrol and placed beneath. This traditional tank crewman's bodge up made a perfectly good cooker that was built afresh each time we stopped. We ate only compo, (composite rations) and our favourite delight was "All in Lob" which was made up of half a dozen tins of anything from suet pudding to fruit or biscuit thrown, 'lobed' into the Dixie and heated through, our culinary abilities were not world renowned.

As with our previous long range patrol we met up with a great deal of resistance from local tribesmen, which came mainly in the form of mining our perimeter when we leaguered up for the night. Each morning we made sure that the heavier, more protected vehicles went first in order to save our more vulnerable 'B' vehicles from destruction. Let me tell you, that you would not want to be the driver of a petrol bowser! The British made land mines that the enemy were using were designed to take out a main battle tank and all of our vehicles were much flimsier than that.

As with the first long range patrol, we visited villages and gave out our magic potions to sick people. Not having a clue about medical matters, my role on these occasions was usually as armed escort for the medic.

At one point we stopped at a small Federal Regular Army fort to leave some supplies for the hard pressed local soldiers. They would have owed their allegiance partly to the Federation and partly to the local Sheik. Although we never saw anything, we were told that they carried out shariah punishments there, including, we were told, beheadings and amputations as per Islamic Law.

Night-time in the desert was incredible, the clear unpolluted desert air made viewing the stars an unforgettable experience. I could certainly understand how people fell in love with the desert.

After the patrol my squadron were given two days off to recover our strength and catch up on sleep. So Ron Woods and I decided to go to Steamer Point in Aden to have a look around. On the way back we where hitching a lift from Aden to our camp in Little Aden about 25 miles away. Within minutes a three ton Para Reg truck stopped for us and we jumped in. South Arabia, or as it is now known, The Republic of Yemen, was a war zone. But boys will be boys and we had hitchhiked to the port of Aden to have a look around, drink a coffee and eat some home baked bread at the Tawahi Bakery near Steamer Point. It was during one of our rare off duty spells and Ron was grumbling because it was my idea and he would rather have chilled out in camp.

As the truck approached the beginning of the man made causeway that the British had built across The Bay of Aden at a place called Ma'alla, we drove past a busy Arab market. In the back of the truck Ron and I sat along with a young Para who was riding shotgun. The vehicle was open without its canvas covers, and as we bumped along sitting on the wooden side benches we had a panoramic view of the sea on our left and the rapidly thinning buildings to our right and rear. In the distance to our right and front lay the desert.

  As we passed the last few stalls of the market an Arab man stepped into view shouting and gesticulating, he must have been no more than 30ft away and I noticed him instantly. He seemed to look me straight in the eyes then produced a revolver from his clothing, aimed it straight at me and fired. The speed of our vehicle had taken us another 30 feet in this time. I looked around me at my companions on the truck. Ron was looking down its side at the road racing by beneath the trucks wheels. The Para who was sitting with his rifle across his legs was staring blankly at the road behind us and in the general direction from where the attack had just come from.

"Did you see that?" I demanded to no one in particular. "See what?" Ron replied. "See the fucking rag head that just shot at us," I snarled. Our guardian who now had a look of embarrassment on his face appeared to be taking a more particular interest in the road behind, but of course it was far too late so he changed his manner into an attempt at displaying a cool disinterest. Ron chipped in. "Last time I go fucking anywhere with you," he paused then added. "Bastard!"
No one was hit, but I was 20 years old and it felt

personal. I think the world changed at that moment, but no one noticed.

In the last month or two of our tour things started to hot up even more. With revolts amongst the local police and Federal Regular Army, who now recognized that the British Government were about to leave them high and dry had to show some loyalty to their soon to be, new masters. It got to the point where making out your friends from your enemies was not easy.

Checkpoint Delta which was at the Little Aden end of the causeway was made up of four sandbag bunkers and a couple of old army marquees. There was a barrier across the road which could be lifted in order to allow travellers to continue their journey after being checked for contraband and weapons. The checkpoint was totally isolated and surrounded by desert and salt flats.
In early October, with only just over a month to complete my tour, 2 Troop was given the checkpoint Delta night duty to perform under the leadership of Yorky Creaser. It was a doddle really; all we had to do was man the bunkers and take it in turns to go on the knife edge where vehicles were stopped.
Everything was going well until about 2am when all hell let loose.

There were no vehicles being searched and

everything was quiet when we began taking incoming machine-gun fire from the desert. The checkpoint's flood lighting made us easy targets for our attackers, but all we could see of them was the muzzle flashes and incoming tracer hitting our bunkers and bouncing off the metal lighting towers, showering puffs of dust off the ground around us. Ron Woods shouted, "Turn the fucking lights off." as we all dived for cover. This seemed to me to be an excellent idea. Unfortunately though, no one knew where the switch was. Half of us were returning fire in the general direction of the assault with our SMGs whilst the others were either relocating and setting up the Bren gun or looking for the light switch. At this point one young lad had the idea of shooting the lights out in order to make us less of a good target and proceeded to open fire on the arc lights with his SMG. Yorky went ballistic shouting that there was no f-ing way he was going to pay for the f-ing lights, so we stopped shooting at them.

The incoming fire was incredibly accurate and our SMGs had neither the range nor the accuracy to get anywhere close to our assailants. At that point our Bren joined the action and was immediately effective, the incoming fire stopped. We patrolled out to find the firing point but the attackers had disappeared into the night leaving only their spent cartridges and the wrapper from a mars bar to show where they had been. No one was hit, and we never

133

did find the fucking light switch.

We were told by some smart arse, that Aden was part of the domain of the Queen of Sheba, and it certainly was a magical place. When dealing with soldiers though it is well to remember that they are not impressed by status. One night when his Royal Highness Major Prince Michael of Kent presented himself at the gates of Falase Camp, requesting entry and explaining that he had forgotten to take his ID card with him. The tanky soldier who was on stag answered, "I don't give a shit if you're the Queen of Sheba mate, you don't get through this gate without an ID card." and refused point blank to let his royal highness in. The next day a formal complaint was received from the prince and our Regimental Sergeant Major, Snowy Evans, who was a big man with a shock of pure white hair and an angry looking red face, called the soldier into his office and asked if it was true. The soldier admitted the offence and expected at least to receive a good bollocking, instead of which Snowy smiled and said, "Good lad."

The tour was drawing to a close. I was twenty one years old and had done an enormous amount of growing up in the last year. The feel and smell of Arabia had awoken something in me which was never to go away, a sense of loyalty to my regiment and to my country and a deep and lasting admiration for the army that I was so proud to belong to. Arabia's magic had washed across my life, leaving me a man. I had formed powerful allegiances which were so intense that they had real texture and substance. I could hear and smell them. It was that feeling of belonging to something unique, a club to which every red blooded man wanted to belong.

The British Government's broadcasting of their intention to withdraw from the Protectorate had the effect of galvanising the public against us. Even those that were our allies turned their allegiance. Who could blame them? When we were gone their new masters would make choices based on what people did now. Within three years the harbour would be filled with Soviet war ships and an insidious brutal form of communism would have taken over people's lives. Without the benefit of hindsight, we knew none of this.

The days leading to my return to UK sped by, and finally the day of my departure arrived. It was the 20th of November 1966 and with disembarkation leave in Germany and accrued leave from the past year I was looking forward to nearly three months off. I climbed back on to the old green bus, which still had a great rent in its side from the rocket attack, but now also carried a great many bullet holes and I watched as Little Aden disappeared in the distance behind me. Onward we went in

respectful silence through Silent Valley where our
dead were buried, and onward down the bumpy
road towers to RAF Khormaksar, where I took one
last look back from the window of the VC10 and
then, "ma salaam" Aden.

"Well that's that fucker done with," said Ron, sitting
next to me.
"We are really going to have to teach you some
English Ron," I retorted.
"Fuck that," said Ron.

On arriving at my mum's house in Saint Mary's
Oldham I put down my suitcase and said, "Mum I'm
going for a pint, I'll be back in a couple of hours."
I walked through the murky back streets where my
Mother now lived and down into the town. On Union
Street in the town centre there was a pub with two
sets of steps leading up to its front entrance. As I
walked in there was that reassuring smell of sticky
carpets and stale beer. The bar was dimly lit and I
could hear the buzz of unseen people talking in
another part of the pub. At the bar a large fat man
demanded, "Yes."
"Pint of bitter please," I said.
"How old are you?" the fat man snapped.
"I'm twenty one," I stated indignantly.
"Try down the road, got to be eighteen here,"
shouted the fat man at my back, as I retreated
muttering curses.

Back at the Incident IRA v Army – Tense times

"Right mate," Ron said. "I need to check what these fuckers are up to." indicating with his thumb and glancing at the three Garda officers who had sauntered up to the border thirty or forty yards away, and were now talking to Ron's troop Corporal. "Fucking miraculous how they only ever appear when everything's over and done with." And then, having had another thought on the subject added, "Bit like you really." And he wandered off having given me a two fingered salute goodbye.

The Bigger the Better
They were a mixed group of men who were waiting in the house. Some of them where young and undergoing training and others were grizzled experienced IRA veterans. The little cottage where they met was in the Republic, but had been chosen for its proximity to the border between Donegal and county Fermanagh in Ulster, where the active service unit had planted a huge land mine. There

were enough explosives in the mine to lay waste to a small town never mind blow up a single vehicle. But their quarry was in fact any military or police vehicle that might pass along the road, the intention being to kill everyone inside the vehicle and send a message of IRA dominance along the border. Fortunately the road that they had mined was so little used and in such dangerous proximity to the border, that no one in uniform had passed along it for some time, leastways no one that they had been awake long enough to see. For the past couple of days the unit had split into two teams in order to keep a twenty four hour watch on the road from their observation hide a hundred yards or so inside the Republic. Should the police or army decide to venture there, they need only wait until the vehicle reached the road above the culvert were the mine was hidden and touch the two wires of the command line onto the battery terminals, whoosh, death and destruction.

There was a stir amongst the gathering when their important guest arrived. David O'Connal or Daithi O'Connaill as he liked to style himself was the Provisional IRA's current Chief of Staff and head of the Provisional Army Council. He was probably the most well-known member of the IRA's leadership. A gaunt looking middle-aged man with an outgoing friendly disposition, O'Connell was quite a celebrity in the IRA. He had been badly shot up by the B

Specials during the nineteen fifties border campaign and spent the next twenty years dining out on it. It was to be a brief visit, the leadership needed to keep hands on with the boys at the front. Little did they know that the two donkeys' who were doing the day shift in the hide, had decided to speed things up by trying to entice the army into the trap. O'Connell, who was a well-known womaniser, had a long history of activity in the Carickmore area of county Tyrone. In the near future Sean O'Callaghan, another member of the group would get to know this area as well. Sean was a young man of about nineteen years, a full time volunteer in the IRA. Thus far the only thing he had managed to blow up was his parent's house in county Kerry, for which he was now on the run from the Garda. Sean was later to become an important player in the war against the IRA. But a lot, including murder and treachery had to happen in Sean's life before this came to fruition.

The others present in the cottage were Pat Doherty, the IRA Quartermaster for Donegal and close accomplice of Martin McGuinness, and a volunteer called Ferris who was the bomb maker. Also present were the day shift donkeys, volunteers Sillery and Hoben. Finally there was the Derry man who was a local IRA commander, and the rest were unfamiliar faces from other parts of Ireland, north and south. A pep talk ensued which quickly turned into a narration of derring do, featuring David O'Connell's many scrapes with death during the 1950s border campaign. He liked a captive audience and was not about to miss the opportunity afforded by this one. After what must have seemed like hours of B Special shoot outs and clandestine raids against the hated English. O'Connal retired to God knows where, possibly to start another verbal campaign with some new victims.

It had been several days since Sillery and Hoben had made their first call informing the Army that there was a culvert bomb near the village of Belleek, if they could get the army to go looking for the mine in the place where they had described it, the army's vehicles would pass over its real position and who knows how many would be killed. Their excitement in anticipation of the attack was tinged with fear though. Although their firing point was believed to be well inside the Republic and therefore safe from British Army intrusion, the area was very open and they had had to build a hide in which they were able to keep their movements from prying eyes. The border in these remote areas was to say the least indistinct, and the Brits often inadvertently infringed on the Republic's sovereignty.

There was little chance of the IRA gang being found by the Garda unless someone informed on them. In this deeply republican area, this was not a possibility. But even though their hide was in the middle of a peat bog and well away from any beaten track, the open nature of the country and poor quality of the ground would prove difficult to retreat from after their proposed attack, especially if that attack was to happen in daylight.

A couple of days later the dynamic duo, Hoben & Sillery got the opportunity to show their metal and failed miserably. On the morning of Sunday July the 15th a surprise assault came in from two British Army helicopters containing seven soldiers from "A" Squadron armed with SLR assault rifles, and one rather scruffy intelligence soldier in jeans and dirty red T shirt armed with a sub machine gun, showing several days' growth of beard and an unruly mop of hair. I looked more like an extra from Mad Max than a serving soldier. Having spent most of the previous two nights in an observation post watching the road I was knackered and not in the best of moods. The dynamic duo's attempt at enticing the army's interest by making telephone calls had backfired and an intelligence led operation had been in the planning for a number of days.

Hoban & Sillery initially attempted to flee carrying their weapons. Realising that this made them legitimate targets for the pursuing soldiers, and not having the courage to take them on in a fire fight, they dropped their M1 rifles and attempted to escape further into the Republic across the peat bog.

The operation had begun around the 8th July when we started receiving anonymous telephone warnings of a bomb on a country road which travelled between Ballynaghra and Trigannon, close to the small town of Belleek. In more peaceful times Belleek is famous for its fine pottery, but to us it was a dangerous border town and prone to attack from the neighbouring Republic. The alleged site of the bomb was on a road that crossed the border into the Republic. We recognised an obvious trap. The calls were very specific about the exact position of the bomb.

Bombs were being found and dealt with by the ATO every week, some weeks several of these devices were found in our area of responsibility that consisted of L and M police divisions. These two divisions covered 1800 square miles of Ulster, the whole of county Fermanagh, and the south western half of county Tyrone. All of the most dangerous border areas barring Armagh fell within our area of control. Some of the IEDs (Improvised Explosive Device) that we came across were as small as a few ounces, made up into letter bombs. And others were huge. A few were enormous, one thousand lb plus.

Because of the proximity of the border, the place they specified was only accessible one way, and that way would take us over a great many drainage culverts where another bomb might be hidden. It was obvious to us that the real bomb was to be found in one of those and that someone at the end of a command wire would be waiting for us to pass down the road. So the plan we hatched was to ignore their calls, which we did for several days. We figured that a few miserable wet days and nights on the end of their command wire should soften them up.

On the tenth day, seven men from "A" Sqn 1RTR and me as int- rep (Intelligence representative) went in by chopper. We started systematically searching both sides of the road from the air. Suddenly two men broke cover from their hide and started running. They were trailing rifles, which they dropped as they ran. They believed that the position of their hide was within the borders of the Irish Republic, and that we would not cross. In fact the border in that area was indistinct. Maybe they were and maybe they weren't. But they were trying to kill us with their bomb, and they were armed. Even by our one-sided rules of engagement we could shoot them both dead.

They were running away in order to get further into the Republic, but their progress was hampered by the sodden peat bog that they were crossing. We exited the hovering aircraft and took chase across the bog.

A big SCOUSE corporal was the first to catch one

143

fleeing terrorist and he brought him down and started hammering into him with fists and boots. I got there seconds later and intervened before he was able to do further damage to the prisoner. By this time we had captured the other one and they were dragged back to the hide where we had first detected them. Nearby we found their weapons, two American M1 carbines. Inside the hide was a scene of domestic bliss, with bits of food and rubbish strewn everywhere. There were batteries and a long wire, leading from the hide across the bog to a drainage culvert which passed under the road. We had found our bomb.

Men from a Royal Engineers search team who had been standing by were sent to check all the other culverts for further bombs, but none were found. They had put all their eggs in one murderous basket. We settled down to wait for Ron Becket to arrive from Omagh with his bomb disposal team.
Charles Hoben, the terrorist who was the first to be caught was in a bad way from his beating. Noal Sillery was pretty much in one piece. So indicating my gun and looking as sinister as I could, I suggested to him that he might wish to dismantle his bomb and pull it out of the culvert, in order to avoid getting his 'fucking head blown off.' He took up my suggestion and when he had completed his task he posed, with a little urging, standing on top of the bomb for photographs. This act of tyrannical

abuse saved the ATO from having to dismantle a potential booby trap.

Sillery, the more experienced volunteer, got thirteen years in prison for his work, and even today is a leading member of the Republican Movement. Hoben got ten years for planting the bomb, which was over a thousand pounds in weight and the largest one to be found in Northern Ireland at that time. The weapons that the pair was carrying were later linked to other shootings in the province. We moved the bomb away from the road in preparation for the ATO to destroy it with a controlled explosion. It was another two hours before the Royal Engineers search team was able to declare the route open to the general public to drive safely through and Ron Becket had detonated the huge 1000lb bomb safely in the peat bog, without damage to the road. The two men were separated and I took charge of Hoben whom I accompanied to Omagh in the back of a police Land Rover, where I signed him over to the Royal Ulster Constabulary. We chatted a little on the way to his inevitable incarceration, and feeling sorry for him in his beat up condition, I gave him a couple of cigarettes and he told me that he was from Dublin.

The trap that they had set was well thought out but made obvious by their impatience to spring it, If they had simply waited, eventually some unsuspecting police or army patrol would have come along and been wiped out. There would certainly have been a significant loss of life.

During my research for this document I spoke at length to Sean O'Callaghan, an ex provisional commander, who as a young volunteer was part of this bomb conspiracy. Sean told me the men that we caught were the day shift. There were three other men including Sean himself who watched over the trap each night. We of course had no idea how close we came to David O'Connell.

As Chief Of Staff of the Provisional IRA and as their leader he would have made a very important capture for us. Certainly worth an impromptu covert visit into the Republic in order to remove him! Someone once said that I would have liked David; he was friendly, amiable and a decent man. Wrong! I would have loved to see David O'Connell spending the rest of his miserable life in an English jail. This would have been just reward for a man whose sole contribution to humanity was the invention of the car bomb. The world wide cost of which in human lives, must by now be in the tens of thousands, not to mention the untold misery caused by the horrific injuries that these devices have inflicted.

It must have been round about this time that during briefings about the current threat, a new boy, who was thought to be operating in our area came into focus. He was a slim young lad, from Cork, about eighteen years of age, the previously mentioned, Sean O'Callaghan. Sean was on the run from the Garda and was believed to be part of an active service unit in west Tyrone. We didn't have a photograph of this young tearaway but he was thought to be a full time volunteer with the Mid Ulster Brigade. The only real information that we had about him being that he had accidently blown up his family home and that of a neighbour whilst polishing up on his bomb making skills. We of course found this to be highly amusing and categorised this newcomer along with other less skilled opponents such as the terrorist that we fondly called Cinders. This would-be terrorist gained notoriety by bodging up an arson job when he poured petrol on his way into a building and then igniting it while he was still inside.

It was a mistake to think of Sean in this way. He turned out to be an astute, thinking man. His abilities as an organiser soon brought him to the attention of the Provisional's leadership and sometime in 1974 he was tasked to take over as leader of the large part time Active Service unit in Carickmore. Although we had crossed swords previously during Sean's training when he was part of the Hoben/Sillery bomb plot near Belleek, this move brought us into direct contention with him. It was noticeable that incidents of all kinds peaked in quantity and intensity in this area during his time of leadership.

As a terrorist Sean was a great success, he did whatever his masters told him to do and completed each task with such skill and tenacity that it became very obvious to us that things had changed and the IRA were upping their game. But as a man Sean was starting to have niggling doubts about his actions and those of some of his fellow volunteers. It wasn't that he had changed his mind about the general aims of his republican beliefs; it was more a dawning suspicion that the IRA was completely sectarian and full of hatred in its outlook. As time went by those doubts would become an obsession with him and start to torment his very existence.

During a massive IRA attack on the Deanery at Clogher, Sean was drafted in to operate the highly unreliable and dangerous homemade mortars, the use of which was to be part of the attack strategy. Thanks to an absconding helper who was supposed to be spotting for him, none of the mortar bombs actually hit the building although the other elements of the attacking force scored a great deal of damage including a large number of RPG 7 rocket strikes which entered and devastated the building. This along with a heavy impact of machine gun fire made for an uncomfortable time for the 1RTR and UDR occupants. Sadly there were casualties including one dead UDR woman, but as stated none from the mortar bombardment.

The aftermath of this event was probably a turning point for Sean. Some of the comments that he had heard from his fellow republicans included one person commenting that it was a great pity that the young UDR woman who'd been killed wasn't pregnant because they would have got two for the price of one, and this comment having come from a Catholic priest. It was therefore a man in turmoil who later, on the 23rd Aug 1974, walked into Broderick's bar in Omagh and fired his gun into Special Branch inspector, Peter Flanagan. Sean then reloaded his empty weapon and fired a further two rounds into the back of his head, causing him to die almost instantly.

This event was like a giant butterfly beating its enormous wings; it completely changed the direction of my life, and probably saved it. Peter Flanagan was my point of contact in Omagh and would have been Controller of my proposed spying activities when I left the army. If Sean had not killed Peter Flanagan, I would have gone off to fight my undercover war in Ireland and would probably have been killed off very quickly. But as yet none of these events had come to fruition and after Sean's catastrophic start as a terrorist; we found it difficult taking him too seriously.

The building that we were mounting our surveillance operation from was in the centre of Omagh and had good views of the area in front of the court house where the demonstration was to take place. The speaker for the evening march and gathering was a republican woman called Myra Drum, a fiery speaker and therefore likely to attract a good crowd. I was with Dinger and we were watching out of the first floor windows of an old building on Market Street that gave us an excellent view of the area that was to be used for the speeches. As usual we made sure that the speakers would have their backs to us in our hideaway, so that our photographs of the crowd would give us a view of their faces. Those kind of activities where invaluable to us, but the bulk of the work would begin the following day when we attempted to put names, to the faces on the photographs that we had won.

This type of job was easy for us. There was no discomfort or danger involved and we would spend the complete evening chatting and getting the occasional photograph. The photography wasn't that challenging, because the street lighting in the town was excellent and we were less than thirty feet from our hiding place to where the speeches were to take place.
  During the course of the evening Mike Mullen dropped in to see how things were progressing and

pointed out a few of the faces that he was particularly interested in, before once again doing his disappearing trick.

I had known Dinger Campbell, my partner on this operation, for a few years now and we had always got along well. He was of medium height with fair curly hair and had a very relaxed, easy going personality. When the demonstration had dispersed, we packed up and headed back in the direction of the camp, dropping in on one of the pubs on route for a drink. The pub that we chose was on Bridge Street and was a favourite squaddie haunt. There was a small narrow bar on the ground floor, dimly lit with a faint aroma of the nearby River Drumragh.

  The people of the town had a certain charm and a kind of old fashioned courtesy which I found very endearing. "Who knows," I thought. "When this lot's done with, I would like to come back here again." I will have a fondness for the town of Omagh.

Border Incident

During this period there were a great many incidents involving homemade explosives. The IRA Mid Ulster Brigade, who was very active in our area, manufactured over two tons of explosive each week in just one of its bomb factories. It is likely that there were other establishments on the go at any one time. We occasionally found and took them out of operation, but it was an easy matter for them to discover a new location and start up production again. The low explosive Anfo was manufactured from high grade nitrate fertiliser rendered down in water and mixed with other substances.

The description Low Explosive refers to the speed at which the ANFO burns during ignition, it does not in any respect mean inferior. Low explosive burns somewhat slower than high explosives and a good mix will give a different but often equal effect. Although there were all manner of government regulations that were supposed to cut down on the availability and purchase of the high nitrate fertilisers used for the manufacture of ANFO, the

IRA with the help of farmers in the Republic always found ways around them and therefore had a constant supply of bomb making material in large quantities.

On one day in particular I was at the scene of an explosion that had killed two soldiers. They had been on patrol in their Land Rover when they were ambushed near to Aughnacloy. The patrol had been travelling down a country lane which ran parallel with the border, when the bomb, which had been hidden in a culvert beneath the road, exploded killing both men and spreading their body parts over a large area in the usual obscene fashion. When I arrived on the scene a search for further explosive devices had already taken place but with negative results so I joined the police dog handlers who were already searching for evidence. We laid the victims bodies by the road side to facilitate their later retrieval, and covered them with large sheets of plastic. It was uncertain that we had found all of the remains, so we kept on searching for evidence because occasionally IRA bomb makers would leave finger prints on the sticky tape that they'd used during the manufacture of these IEDs. Even after this tape had been at the centre of a massive explosion it was sometimes possible to retrieve the person's finger prints as evidence against the bomb maker.

One very young looking police officer was calling his dog which had vanished into the undergrowth, but the animal was too interested in something that he had found there. Eventually the dog reappeared carrying in its mouth what was obviously some part of one of the victim's body. The piece, which was ten or eleven, inches long and three or four inches in diameter, had no skin and was unrecognisable. We checked the find by scrutinizing it from every conceivable angle but were still clueless to which part of the victim's anatomy it had belonged.

The police officer bagged the grisly remains in a transparent polythene evidence bag and continued with the search. We spent the next two hours combing the undergrowth without further success. Then the Police officer walked over to me and in an excited manner proclaimed that he knew what it was. I stopped what I was doing and straightened up to see him vigorously bending the mortal remains in the bag "It's an arm," he said triumphantly. I looked at it curiously, and yes, I thought, take the hand and remove most of the wrist, sever it from the arm just above the elbow and completely skin it, and that's what we had got. Incredible as it may seem, I felt a kind of warm satisfaction at our having resolved the mystery.

Subsequently I speculated a lot about the damage we must all be suffering psychologically. Being constantly bombarded with these grisly horrific images day in and day out could not be good for us. Often the victims of these attacks were people that we knew. Some of those police officers and UDR soldiers subsequently spent the whole of their careers putting up with these kinds of mind warping events and ended up with debilitating Post Traumatic Stress Disorder, and little else to show for it.

Whenever a major incident occurred there would be a gathering of experts and others whose job it would be to make the scene safe or collect evidence against the perpetrators of the crime. For instance our ATO would stand by just in case any bombs were found. Police scene Of Crimes Officers or Special Branch would attend and usually the army's PR department would be present. It was normal to use explosives sniffer dogs to check out the area before the gathering took place in case any presents had been left for us by the IRA. Everyone got on with their individual jobs but as time went by these gatherings became almost social events. It was usually the same people who gathered and they all knew each other, and were more or less on first name terms.

This group of friends suffered a high casualty rate and of the fifteen or so regular members four of them had lost their lives in separate incidents within just over one year. The amount of death and carnage that we had to handle on a daily basis forged some powerful friendships and subsequently left ragged holes in already damaged lives when members of our close group where murdered.

Bomb Squad

The EOD Section or Bomb Disposal Team in Omagh was the most active in the UK (if not in the world at that time) in terms of the quantity of devices, and tonnage of explosives that we were dealing with. According to Sean O'Callaghan in his excellent book *The Informer*, during late '73-early '74 the Provisional's were manufacturing a minimum of two tons of homemade explosive every week solely for use in our area. Our team was made up of one Ammunition Technical Officer (ATO) and about six other guys who drove the vehicles or provided armed cover for the ATO when he was working on a device. When an ATO was present at the scene of a bomb, no matter what rank of the others present, he was in control. An important role was also played by the explosive sniffer dog handlers and their animals. Notable amongst which was the long serving team of Brian Criddle and his dog Jason. As a group, and along with police and Special Branch officers, we always attended the bombing and shooting incidents.

Our bomb disposal team were all familiar with the equipment used including the oddly named Wheelbarrow. A typical bug-out would involve the loading of one vehicle with equipment and a long wheelbase civilian style Land Rover with bench seats and windows, which acted as a crew cab. Often the Land Rover would be towing a trailer in which Wheelbarrow was moved around the countryside. Wheelbarrow was the name given to the earliest robotic tracked vehicle to be used for bomb disposal, anywhere in the world. It was at that time brand new to the British Army. Wheelbarrow MK1 was developed by Lieutenant Colonel Peter Miller, who built a hybrid EOD vehicle from an electric wheelbarrow and a lawn mower in his garden shed. After further development the vehicle came into service in late1972. After extensive further development and after it was armed with CCTV and adapting remote control it was possible to manipulate its robotic arm and hand in order to place a disruptive charge, or initially inspect a suspected IED. It was also possible to mount a 12 bore shotgun on the arm. The shotgun fired solid shot which had a considerable disruptive effect on any bomb that it was aimed at. Wheelbarrow MK1 was very much an experimental vehicle, and was the forerunner of the much more sophisticated EOD robots of today.

The ATO was the team leader and normally he

would be the only member to approach the bomb in order to work on it. Some ATOs were more relaxed about this rule than others. But usually he was the only man to take that long lonely walk. Staff Sergeant Ron Beckett was the only ATO in my experience who didn't mind others slightly sharing the risks. On one occasion

n we had a spate of letter bombs, there were six in one day.

Another bomb attack

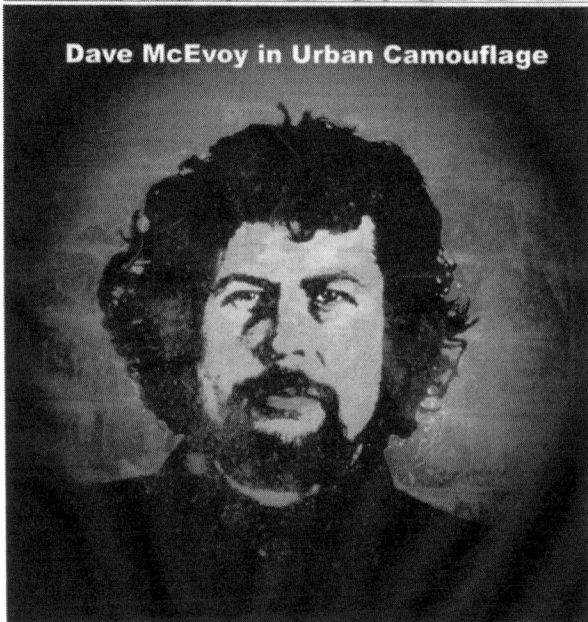
Dave McEvoy in Urban Camouflage

At one of the houses that we visited the recipient had recognised that there was something odd about his copy of the *Reader's Digest* that he had received in the morning post. Not least the fact that he didn't subscribe to that journal. So he placed the suspicious package on the lawn in front of his house and waited for the ATO to arrive. Ron cut the book containing the explosives out of its envelope and was holding it open on the lawn for me to photograph. As long as the pages of the book was wide open it was safe, but if it closed and the aluminium foil contacts on the pages touched together the bomb would explode.

Ron moved his hands out of the way of my camera as I leaned over to get my shot when suddenly a breath of wind blew the pages closed. My reaction was immediate. I doubt that I could have moved faster if I had a rocket stuck up my backside. I covered the area of the lawn in two giant strides and turned to see if it had gone off. I was met by a silence interrupted only by Ron rolling around the lawn laughing; for some reason the connection made by the two pieces of foil was not good enough and the necessary circuit did not complete. Sadly Ron was killed by a booby trap within a few weeks of this incident.

During the tour I worked with about six different ATOs and classed them as the most courageous men

I have ever met. Each and every day they risked their lives. Our enemy went to a great deal of trouble to kill ATOs by means of booby traps and the likes. The risks involved in attending the scene of a bomb didn't just relate to the bomb itself. Sometimes there were other devices hidden and waiting for the unsuspecting soldier or if the bomb was sited near to the border there was a good possibility that you might come under attack by gunfire from volunteers ensconced safely in the Republic. The ATOs team were volunteers from all different regiments. The team always stuck together, and they brought a whole new meaning to the term, 'gallows humour.' They worked together with one aim and that was to keep the boss alive.

23rd July 1973 Cpl Bryan Criddle & Jason

Bryan, an explosives sniffer dog handler and I often met at the scene of incidents. His dog Jason was one of the most experienced explosive sniffer dogs in the Army. On or around the 23rd of July, Brian told me that he was having a small party in the back room of the NAFFI and that I was invited. I asked him what the occasion was but he wouldn't say.

That evening at about eight p.m. six people including Bryan's wife, who I had never met before, gathered in the NAFFI's small back room and started drinking beer. After a few minutes Brian passed me a letter and asked me to read it, saying that this was the reason for the celebration.
  The letter stated that Bryan was to be awarded the British Empire Medal for his and Jason's work relating to sniffing out IEDs over the past three years. Between them they had dealt with hundreds of bombs and suspect devices containing many tons of explosives, and they had been there from the very start of the conflict. I congratulated Bryan and told him that his award was well deserved and couldn't

have gone to a better team. I can remember thinking cynically that someone in higher authority must have made a mistake. Bryan and Jason were real heroes and medals usually only get passed around amongst the officers. This team did one of the most dangerous jobs in the army, day after day, month after month for almost three long years. Brian's family must have been very proud of him. We drank a lot of beer and had a great night.

A big problem for us at that time was the ease with which terrorists crossed the border from the Republic by illegal crossing points, and later used them to escape back from where they came. We had neither the resources nor the manpower to control these crossing points on a regular basis. It made it very easy for them to import explosives and weapons for their campaign, and armed attacks on border villages were becoming more prevalent. Terrorist incursions across the border into the north made up a large percentage of the incidents that we as security forces had to deal with. We constantly had to crater illegal crossing points, or block them with large concrete crocodile's teeth, as they were known, in order to deny their use to the IRA. In doing so we were also blocking the use of these roads to local people who traditionally used the roads to move around locally and since the separation of Northern Ireland from the Republic their use expanded into that of two- way smuggling routes. We, as security forces, took no interest in the smuggling as long as it didn't include the importation of weapons and explosives. Later in the campaign though, the revenue from these activities supplied a lot of the IRA's funding.

It must be added that weapon systems used by both the IRA and the prod extremist groups were either donated or purchased with funds from abroad. The IRA had extensive links with other terrorist organisations around the world and found benefactors' in such people as Omar Gadaffy who helped fuel the conflict by supplying arms directly and the funding for the purchase of armaments and explosive components. Whenever money for that purpose ran low, the IRA would refill their coffers by committing bank and post office robberies, though most of the money gained in that way never got any further than the back pockets of the perpetrators'.

The influential Irish American community collected vast amounts of money which they thought was going towards the beleaguered Catholic communities in the north. Most of this in fact went directly to the IRA to facilitate the deepening and lengthening of the armed conflict. Noraid funding also came in useful, especially for the purchase of American weapons as the assets were often collected in the USA which cut out the increasing difficulty that they had in movement of those funds. In the early days of the campaign much of the weaponry purchased came direct from the US but as time passed by the American authorities tightened up hard on those activities, nevertheless, they were never able to stop them completely.

The IRA's later acquisition and use of sniper technology towards the latter end of their operations brought a particularly sickening and tragic conclusion to their campaign. Not for the first time a conspiracy of silence descended upon the politicians as it was believed that both the weaponry and possibly the manpower involved came from the United States.

Around about the date of Bryan's party we received intelligence that on the 27th of July, PROVOs from the Republic were going to reinstate one of the main crossing points at Loughmore on the Tyrone/Monaghan border close to the village of Clogher. I was sent the night before as part of an observation team. We were dropped off about a mile away and walked in to our OP position under the cover of darkness. At about 2 a.m., during our march in, and as we got closer to the border, I kept getting a whiff of ANFO. I commented that there was a big bomb somewhere nearby. It was very late when we arrived at a suitable location for our OP. I was dressed in civvies and carrying my camera equipment and a knackered old sleeping bag that I had borrowed from the stores. The night was very cold for the time of year and by morning I was shivering hard and wondered how the hell I was going to use the three-foot long telephoto lens which would need a steady hand. Shortly after first light they arrived.

There were about seventy people, mainly men, but some women as well. They started moving things around and widening the track with shovels to bypass the area of cratering. They appeared to be moving other things around but it was difficult to see from our position exactly what they were actually doing. As I watched them a feeling came over me that there was something amiss. A group of them were visually exploring the surrounding hills and appeared to be discussing things of an urgent nature between each other. Although we had gone to a great deal of trouble to keep our presence covert, they were acting as if they knew we were there. I believe to this day that we were seeing the setting of a very sophisticated trap. It was difficult from where we where to make out what these people where doing but they were moving things around as well as repairing the road. It turned out later that what they were setting up was a circle of bombs hidden in the undergrowth. The ease with which the Intel had come to us, plus the presence of the very aggressive rent a mob made it likely that this was a planned trap.

Within minutes the scouts that they had dispatched had found us. They had sent out half a dozen men to search the fields and hedgerows until they discovered us in the drainage ditch on the hillside overlooking the crossing point. We quickly packed away our equipment in order to bug out, but as soon as the call went up from the scouts a mob of people came quickly up the hill to confront us. The danger of their act being, if we allowed this large aggressive crowd to get in amongst us, there was a strong possibility that their weight of numbers might help them to overpower our small group and use our weapons against us. The section of men that I was with was commanded by a corporal who assessed the situation and told us in a loud voice to stand our ground and aim our weapons at the leading elements of the mob that were by now only fifteen feet away from us.

The feelings that were going through my head at that time where, in a sentence, that it all came down to two things, can I shoot an unarmed stranger, and if I find that I can't, will it cost me my life?

I was having difficulty keeping my Browning pistol aimed straight. My body's core temperature must have been very low and I was shaking hard. I stood aiming my browning at the crowd of advancing republicans knowing that my civilian clothes

pointed me out as a hated army spy. They knew that our yellow card (each soldier had to carry with him a yellow card with rules of engagement detailed on it) would not allow us to fire unless we were shot at first. Of course they didn't need to shoot at us; if they got amongst us they could kill us all with our own weapons. Take our weapons out of the equation by means of the yellow card, and we were outnumbered more than ten to one. At this point the patrol commander, Glyn Buckley, pointed out one of the leading men in the still advancing mob, and in a voice which they could all hear, said. "The man in the white shirt, if they take one more step shoot him in the chest," and then quickly added, "everyone."
The whole situation instantly changed. They froze to the ground. The command was convincing, and the thought of four seven point six two and one nine millimetre bullets slamming into the chest of their obvious leader unnerved all of them.

When we backed off and started walking out they were howling and jeering at us but they still didn't move. As we got a little further away from the mob, carrying all our equipment, we ran into Mike Mullen who had been watching the confrontation through binoculars from about a quarter of a mile away. Mike, who was leaning against a Q car, gave Glyn a well deserved slap on the back for his excellent handling of the situation.

My part in the operation had come to an end, I went back to camp with Mike and hit the sack to get some well-earned sleep. I was due to go on leave the next day. Later in the day I dropped into the intelligence cell to catch up on the operation and was told what had happened next.

It appeared that we had, without realising it, been watching the IRA set up this deadly trap. The whole thing had been staged in order to entice us into an ambush. Shortly after we extricated ourselves, "C" Sqn arrived at the crossing and the mob crossed into the Republic to watch Bryan Criddle and his dog Jason sweep the area to check for booby traps, before work could begin on disrupting the crossing point again. Bryan and the patrol from "C" Sqn walked straight into the trap. A circle of hidden milk churns and some large plastic bags of Anfo, each with a hundred + lb of explosive in each were laid in a necklace of death. The device was detonated by means of command wire by the jeering IRA mob who where ensconced safely in the Republic. The planned chain reaction failed and luckily only a small part of the ring of death actually exploded. If it had all gone off to plan, up to twenty soldiers would have been killed.

As it was, Bryan Criddle BEM received severe injuries from which he died five days later. I never heard what happened to Jason, the good natured sniffer dog that was reputed to have more flying hours than any of our two squadrons of helicopter pilots. Jason's acute sense of smell was confused by the large number of people who had been so recently working on setting this deadly trap and he had led his friend Brian directly into the killing ground. The mob, who were two hundred yards away in the safety of the Republic, where laughing and howling at the fallen hero and as per usual, the Irish authorities where conspicuous by their absence throughout.

With Bryan's death the PROVOs where on a roll and decided to try out what I thought was the lowest, most despicable attack against us so far. On August 9th at 9.20 a.m. they placed a huge proxy bomb in 1RTRs married quarters. A number of women and small children were injured, luckily none of the injuries where severe. No warning was given of the 400lb bomb in a post office van which was stolen and placed on Alexander Rd. This cowardly attack by the IRA against women and children was at 9.20 in the morning when no soldiers would be around. Having heard the explosion from the Int cell I was at the scene within a couple of minutes. The damage caused was quite extensive with about thirty army married quarters taking the brunt of the explosion. Many others had windows blown in. The sunken road where the device exploded was about six feet below the surrounding area where the houses stood. This is probably what saved the lives of those in the houses closest to the blast. The main effects of the blast were directed upwards towards the sky, rather than outwards towards the houses, some of which were less than thirty yards away. Never the less it was little short of a miracle that no one was killed or seriously injured by the four hundred plus pounds of explosives contained within the bomb.

The IRA gave no warning of that bomb, so one can only assume that their intention was to kill the wives and children of the regiment. Whatever the intention of this attack, it failed miserably, although an enormous amount of damage was done to the married quarter's complex, there was no mass exodus of families and the regiment soldiered on with renewed vigour. It is a measure of the professionalism of these soldiers that even after such a disgusting depraved act, they were able to remain focused on their prime objective and not get side tracked into pointless revenge.

Dangerous concealment in a graveyard

On August 11th fate took a hand in balancing the score sheet, Seamus Harvey, an infamous IRA bomber who was currently our No1 target managed to kill himself along with his fellow volunteer Gerard McGlynn while transporting a bomb across the border from Donegal in the Republic to County Tyron. Both of these Castlederg men were on the run from the authorities in the North. I was tasked to do an aerial and ground reconnaissance of the country house where Seamus's wake was being held. My pilot celebrated with his best stab at a victory roll for all Harvey's family and friends that had gathered there.

Harvey had planted a number of very destructive devices during the previous few months including a number in his home village of Castlederg. On the way back to Lisanelly in our two seated Sioux helicopter we discussed the pilots pathetic attempt at a victory role, which had been more of a shuffle from side to side than an actual roll. Having never been very much at home without my feet being placed firmly on the ground, I asked the pilot, a 2nd Lieutenant, what would happen if the engine stopped and then, much to my dismay, he gained a bit more altitude and then demonstrated the result by switching off the engine. As we spiralled towards the ground in silence he informed me that they can sometimes be a bit of a bastard to get started again.

The next day was the day of Harvey's funeral and dawn found me hidden in the graveyard. The rain came down hard, but no surprises there, this was Ulster and the rain always came down hard. Forty shades of dank musty green, with even the height of summer feeling cool. Here I was anticipating the end of another night of shuffling around uncomfortably, waiting for the morning's warming light.

The two, 4 Field Troop soldiers that I was with were more used to this kind of operation than I was and had come prepared in good waterproof equipment and ghillie suits. I on the other hand was wearing civvies which were more suitable for a stroll in the countryside than to lying in a rain filled ditch all night; I was cold, damp and more importantly trying to control my shivering. In short, I was wishing like hell that this long night was well and truly over with. I had however learned something from my previous observation posts; I had borrowed a military style parker in an attempt to keep myself a little warmer.

Once in position you would almost stand on us before noticing our presence in the fringes of the overgrown cemetery, but if the rain kept up there would be little chance of my getting the photographs that we had come for. As the night rolled slowly on there appeared a flicker of optimism in the southern sky, so I made my preparations

"Does anyone have any idea what time this funeral is going to happen?" I asked.

"No," Bill answered. "But I think it's today."

"You think it's today," I questioned with a groan. "What if it's not?"

"We wait until it does happen," he stated flatly. The thought of spending more interminable hours, or even days in this soggy hole in the ground, did not amuse me. It's true that we had brought a small amount of food and water with us and somewhere amongst our kit were plastic bags in which we could defecate, if it came to a long wait, but I fancied neither the rations nor the toilet facilities, so I groaned again. As a young soldier I would have almost enjoyed this kind of depravity but now at the grand old age of twenty eight I had grown to enjoy the more luxurious aspects of my existence such as cook house breakfasts and a bed to sleep in at night.

We had moved into our positions during the early hours of the morning, now the first flickering of the new day's dawn was creeping furtively across the fringes of the sullen sky and the rain was easing off a little.

We were to be uninvited guests at a double IRA funeral for Volunteers Seamus Harvey and Gerard McGlynn; both of whom were Castlederg men and had been killed by their own bomb whilst transporting it. The large car bomb that they were driving from the Republic, in order to attack their home town, self detonated when they stopped to have a fiddle with it at the border. Their demise had occurred a few days earlier on the 11th of August and I had already paid that flying visit the previous day to their wake, courtesy of one of our choppers, and was now in the process of preparing to extend my photo album of the occasion.

The funerals of the two men would constitute a fine opportunity for me to get up to date photographs of some of the newer players in the game. Of course the IRA would know that and would expect us to try to use the funeral for intelligence gathering purposes. It was therefore a risk; they would know for certainty that we would be there. There was no realistic chance of help for us if anything went wrong; our extraction team were about a mile away from the grave yard, so we were on our own.

All three of us were crammed like sardines into a shallow depression in the ground on the heavily overgrown fringes of the burial area with bushes to our front and sides. The lads were practically invisible in their "ghillie" suits and lay on either side of me. All of us were covered by a cam net with lots of fabric tags and pieces of foliage retrieved from the local area woven into it, leaving only a small thin patch for my camera lens to shoot through. As the sky started to lighten even more we kept perfectly still and silent.

It was shortly after first light when we heard the voices. Initially it was just a murmur, then getting louder as they approached. I wasn't able to tell what they were saying, nor was I able to see them. Bill indicated that they were somewhere behind us and moving in our direction along the cemetery's boundary fence. As they got closer, we were able to pick up individual words and phrases in their conversation and it appeared that they were looking for something - or was it someone? The thought crossed my mind that maybe it was us. Within a few moments we could hear them distinctly. There were two men and they were within a few feet of us, so we lay perfectly still until their noises and movements had passed us by.

 I was cold, wet and stiff but at least the rain had stopped and the day had started to brighten up a bit. We hadn't actually seen our visitors, but knew from the scraping of their feet and sound of their voices

177

that they had come within a few feet of where we were hiding and they never had discovered us. This added greatly to my feeling of security, but an hour or so later they were back.

Our view from the hide was limited by the bushes to our front and by the overgrown grave yard around us. On arriving the previous night one of the 4 Field Troop lads had made a search of the area for the two freshly dug graves before a decision was made as to the position of our hide. It was decided that it was impractical for us to overlook the burial area, so we had chosen a position adjacent to the footpath which led down to that end of the burial ground. This position would enable me to get shots of the mourners as they proceeded to the newly dug graves carrying the coffins.

The sound of men shouting came from further up the small burial ground, but there was no real urgency in their calls that might have indicated that we were in trouble, so we just stayed perfectly still and alert. I had started to feel a bit more comfortable and the shivering had subsided as the day warmed and after preparing the old Pentax camera with its standard 50mm lens, I pulled my pistol from its hip holster, cocked it and let it rest on the damp grass next to my camera and between my outstretched hands. It was difficult to hear what the raised voices were saying due to the thick accents of the men and their distance from us, but it seemed like one of them was giving instructions.

They were right on top of us before we were able to see them. Six, possibly eight men were in search formation, some of them beating the undergrowth with sticks and diligently searching the grave yard and its overgrown fringes. We could see six, but more voices came from behind us. Shit! I thought, these were bad lads and they were getting very close to finding us. We were not able to see any weapons, but the confidence of their search made me think that it was likely that some of them would be armed.

Two members of their team where now within ten feet of us and we could hear the swish of the sticks that they were using to disturb the long grass and bushes. How could they not see us? One man in particular stood for two or three minutes, only four or five yards in front of us, visually searching the boundary fence area. I could have got a good close up of his face, but the thought of the shutter noise stopped me and I clutched my Browning pistol tighter instead.
The voice of their director of operations, who was a thick set man with a ruddy complexion and scruffy, greying red hair, sent them to some bushes further down the path and they moved on without disturbing us.

The search took about fifteen minutes and when they had completed it to their satisfaction, all of the men, once again disappeared and shortly afterwards the funeral procession appeared on the gravel path. The two coffins were covered in tricolour flags, with family and friends following close behind. The coffins were being carried by male family members and other men who we thought were volunteers from their Active Service Unit. Our closeness to the activities made it easy to get the best shots through a gap in the bushes as the sixty or more mourners moved down the path a few yards to our front and to an area hidden from us, where the interments were to take place.

I had enough photographs by now and the job was complete so we just waited motionless and in silence. It was now just a matter of time before the proceedings were completed and the cemetery would empty. We could then call in our extraction team and bug out of this god dammed place, what could go wrong?

Although the funeral cortege were now out of our sight, their mumbled prayers where still audible to us in our hide. There was a momentary silence then shots rang out as they directed the murderous souls of the deceased on their way to Provo heaven. My body stiffened at the sound of the shots. I thought for a split second that we had been discovered, but soon realized that what I was listening to was the customary salute to the dead volunteers from the other members of their active service unit. But the noise of the shots finally answered the question in our minds as to whether or not there were any weapons amongst the mourners.

It was not the army's policy to turn every IRA funeral into a bloody pitched battle whenever weapons were produced, so we kept quiet and held our peace. When the funeral service was completed, groups of mourners made their way back up the burial area moving from left to right, and across our front. It was another chance which I gladly took to get more photographs.

The groups turned to a trickle, and finally three small boys took up the rear. The last one came within inches of standing on my outstretched hand, beneath the cam net. We gave it another couple of hours and then pulled out leaving everything as near as possible as we found it, and were picked up by an old Transit van on a nearby track.

The boys dropped me off back at Lisanelly where I just collapsed on my bed and fell asleep thinking, Shit that was close! And wondering where I could get one of those ghillie suits?

Those special camouflage suits that 4 Field Troop used were like sniper suits, designed to break up the outline of a soldiers body by using more material than is used in the manufacture of normal camouflage clothing. The suit or overalls are covered in fabric tags in camouflage colours, of various lengths, which further blur and hide the shape of the human body. The use of these ghillie suits, as we called them, made a soldier almost invisible against a woodland or grassy scrubland background. The ghillie suit's usefulness was limited to surveillance duties because, although they were excellent at hiding a soldier's presence in rural areas, the suit constricted his movement and was therefore difficult for him to move around and use weapons and equipment in.

Derived from the Gaelic word for servant, a Scottish ghillie was a helper during a deer hunt. The suit bearing the same name was developed originally in Scotland for the purpose of endowing its wearer with extreme close up camouflage. The suits first known military use was by the British Army during the Boer war and they have gone on to be used by specialized military units and hunters all over the world. The manufacture of these suits is often accomplished by the soldier who is to be the suit wearer himself and differs in use of materials and colours dependent on the nature of terrain that it is to be used in. From open desert to close woodland, the ghillie suit can offer the soldier a degree of invisibility not attainable by any other means.

The suit is constructed by hand from natural

materials found in the environment in which the suit is to be used and enhanced by the addition of sacking or jute flaps of suitably blended colours and can take a great deal of time to get right. When you consider that the life of the suit wearer is often dependent on its quality of build, it is of no surprise that a soldier will often spend weeks getting its look right. In the context of covert operations in Ireland, the suit's use held no major drawbacks other than their bulky nature but in other parts of the world there are limitations caused by extremes of temperature and climate.

 Within two weeks of this incident the IRA proved that they were still in business in that area by attacking the long suffering Castlederg community with two bombs on August the 23rd.
Two car bombs exploded; one outside a bar on Main St and the other bomb 30 minutes later. There was a 1 minute warning of the first bomb. The second bomb was meant to kill anyone attracted to the scene by the warning of the first explosion. Staff Sergeant Ron Beckett the ATO gave me a lift from Omagh to the scene of the incident where I spent most of the day photographing damage and sitting in on interviews of witnesses with DC John Doherty in the police barracks.

Staff Sergeant Ron Beckett neutralising a letter bomb with a controlled explosion. On this particular day we visited several sites where these devices had been successfully delivered.

Tullyhomman Post Office

On the morning of 30th August, Ron was called out to a number of suspected bombs in the border village of Pettigo. A gang of IRA volunteers had driven across the border from the Republic into Pettigo and proceeded to shoot the village up. The gang then collected some of the villagers together and started questioning them. One local boy was shot whilst trying to get away. They took the names and addresses of people as well as questioning them about their religious beliefs. Meanwhile other gang members planted two large bombs.

Mervin Johnston, one of the villagers, who was also a member of the part time Ulster Defence Regiment recognised that the religious questioning might be leading to some kind of an atrocity and decided to take action. Mervin courageously fought with one of the armed men and ran under fire to his home. He collected his Sterling sub machine gun which he kept in his property and took on the gang single handed in a fire fight which lasted a few minutes before the gang took to their heels returning fire as they escaped back across the border into the Republic. The boy who was shot survived his injuries.

It was a warm pleasant summer's day when the news came through about the bombing and shootings that were taking place in Pettigoe. I was sitting in the back of the Bomb Squad's crew Land Rover that would be taking us to the scene of the incident after Ron's Bomb disposal team had finished loading the other Land Rover. I had taken off my jacket to alleviate the heat in the vehicle somewhat, and was now sat with my shoulder holster and Browning pistol in view.

Ron who was sitting in the front of the vehicle said. "Give me your camera a minute, Dave." and explained. "I'll take a photograph for your grand kids."

Handing over the camera, I answered. "You do know the front from the back end of that thing, don't you?" (Meaning the camera) "I know you're crap with technical things."

"You remember that letter bomb that he was supposed to be holding open for you to photograph?" one of the team said.

"I let that go on purpose," Ron stated. "I needed to see if you could really move that fast!" Everyone except me was laughing; I just looked at them with a sickly expression on my face. After taking the photograph he said.

"Anyway the lads are ready, time to go see what Paddy has in store for us," and we were once more off down the familiar road from the camp.

About 40 minutes later we arrived to deal with the remaining bomb. Of the two bombs that the IRA had left us; during the time that we were travelling to the incident, one had exploded destroying the local garage, so on arrival we were able to concentrate on the remaining device. After Ron had reconnoitred the post office where the remaining bomb was located he asked me to go to the doorway of the shop and photograph a suspicious looking pile of sacks that were leaning against the far wall of its interior. There was something about the way everything had been moved around in there that had started warning bells ringing in Ron's head. He decided that he didn't like the sacks that were leaning against, and along the far wall opposite the entrance to the shop. He felt they may hide a booby-trap device
.

The inside of the shop looked to me like an old fashioned feed store; it was dark and had a strange odour which I couldn't quite put my finger on. I knew one thing though; one ingredient of that smell was ANFO. With no obvious sign of the bomb inside I guessed it to be hidden behind the sacks which had been placed against the far wall and with my photographs taken, I quickly left. The answer to dealing with this device, Ron decided, was to move the bulging sacks using a long piece of cord with a hook on the end (known to us as a hook & line). Once he had hooked the sack, he was able to move it by pulling the line from a safer distance so that if this resulted in the triggering of the bomb he would be at least 40 yards away from the heart of the resulting explosion. This distance, plus the cover that he had taken behind one of our Land Rovers and the protection afforded by his bomb protection suit plus visor, would hopefully be enough to protect Ron from both the blast and the flying debris.

Having moved part of the potential booby-trap with his hook and line to no effect, Ron decided to wait for a statutory half an hour in order to be sure that the bomb had no delay mechanism which might catch him out. I sat on the low wall opposite, further down from where the Post Office was situated, and waited for Ron to make his next move. Thinking to myself that this may take all day, if I got the chance I would scrounge a lift back to Lisanelly. Meanwhile, for some reason beyond comprehension, Ron had decided to take another look in the Post Office. Under those kinds of circumstances it was normal to wait thirty minutes after moving anything, before approaching the device again. But whether it was to save time or what? I don't know, but Ron decided to have another look.

As he walked in the doorway the bomb went off killing him and blowing his body to pieces. I was lifted by the blast and deposited several yards away in the lee of the wall that I had been sitting on. When I shakily picked myself up I discovered that my clothes and face were covered in a strange slimy gray coating from the building and from Ron. Ron Beckett was a large friendly man, a little over weight if truth be known. Only a small percentage of him was found by the soldiers, police officers and distraught villagers, who had to search for and collect his bits in bin liners around Tullyhomman Post Office, near Pettigo.

Ron's funeral service was held in the camp a few days later, and as I knew him so well I took time out to attend. The manner of his death left everyone shocked and disgusted, but sadly life went on. Within hours a new Staff Sergeant ATO had arrived as his replacement and everything just carried on as if nothing had happened. The only reference Sinead made to this incident was to ask me if I knew the dead ATO, to which I simply answered. "Yes".

Omagh town centre 1973

Bomb Squad and Dave at scene of booby trapped stolen car.

Ammunition Technical Officer (Bomb Disposal) Viewing the scene at Ulster Defence Regiment HQ, destroyed by small IED. This bomb consisted of only about 40lb of commercial explosives.

Destruction of large amount of captured explosives on border with Republic.

A captured IRA Volunteer posing on top of a 1000lb fertiliser bomb that he had planted. This was at the time the largest device to be set in the troubles to date.

'Death of Innocents and Dingers Mini'

On September 5th an incident was reported at Belcoo where a large bomb had exploded under a tractor which was being driven by a young Catholic boy along the Garrison Rd. Patrick Duffy, a farm labourer who was nineteen years old, was killed instantly when the road beneath his tractor disappeared into a fifteen foot deep crater, caused by a mine that had been placed in a culvert that ran under the road. Both the remains of the tractor and the boy's body ended up in the mangled crater. Paddy Carrol and I attended the scene of the atrocity.

We arrived before the army or the police had a chance to search the scene for other bombs. In fact we were the first security forces people at the incident. About a hundred yards away from where the wreckage of the tractor lay, with the body of the boy still lying in it, we found a large box sitting in the middle of the road with the word BOMB written on it. I avoided the temptation to kick the box into the roadside hedge and along with Paddy went to search for the firing point.

The IRA often set more than one bomb in order to kill those who responded to the first explosion with the second one, but it was very unlikely that they would advertise the fact by writing BOMB on the device.

Family members of the dead farm boy, who were present, asked that no photographs be taken of the body which lay at the bottom of a huge crater under the wreckage of the tractor.

It was thought that the wheels of the tractor had been mistaken, as it passed a break in the hedgerow, for those belonging to one of our scout cars by the terrorists who were hidden two hundred yards away. As stated, the fact that the young man who was killed was himself a Catholic, I often wondered at whose door the family laid the blame for his death? We later found the remains of the command line by which the bomb had been detonated.

The line terminated in the Republic, so we had to await the arrival of the Garda in order to get a proper look at the fire position. The boy's body lay in the wreckage of his tractor overnight before being removed the following day. Army commanders thought that there was a lot of potential for the scene to be booby trapped and therefore waited for the availability of a specialised search team from the Royal Engineers before uniformed personnel were allowed anywhere near. Another giant balls up by the volunteers of the Provisional IRA.

The IRA hadn't finished their evil work in the village that week. Two days later 54 year old Mathew Lilley, an off duty UDR soldier, was murdered while delivering milk around the area. Mathew was ambushed by two IRA volunteers who shot him dead at Kellaghoe, near Belcoo. These ordinary men and women of the Ulster Defence Regiment took extraordinary risks in defending their communities against the IRA's murderous attacks. During this bloody campaign, over 200 members of the Ulster Defence Regiment where killed on active service with many more received grievous, life changing injuries. The later prevalence of PTSD (Post Traumatic Stress Disorder) amongst these brave men and women, is in itself an indication of the kind of stresses that that these veterans suffered, in some cases for decades.

Throughout 1973 there was a steady escalation of the bloodshed in the Province and we were becoming expert at piecing together the threads of the IRA's movements. Predicting their activities and countering them, both overtly by means of troop deployments and covertly by other means, became second nature to us.
Shortly before 11 p.m. on a night in mid September I

had driven to the RUC station at Cookstown with Dinger Campbell. We were to debrief that night's patrol commander. The RUC station was a large fortified building on the outskirts of the town and surrounded by country roads. A spike in IRA activity in the area had taken our interest and we felt it to be important to pick up any local intelligence that we could. We were building up a picture in order to predict the direction of future activity in the area. After the patrol commander for the night had been fully debriefed we had spent some time talking to the duty police sergeant before retiring to their on site bar for a swift half before heading back. It was now coming up to midnight when we received a phone call from the operations room at Lisanelly. A bomb had exploded in the bar of the Silver Birch Hotel. The pub was within a short distance of the camp gate in Omagh. The building was set back from the Gortin Road by a large car park and was a favourite haunt of soldiers from the camp, it had recently figured in intelligence, which indicated that the IRA was taking a particular interest in it. Although the explosion had taken place a couple of hours before, we dropped everything and jumped into Dinger's car in order to make a speedy return to Omagh.

Dinger's car, though second hand, had only recently been purchased and was his pride and joy. It was a very smart Mini Cooper S painted in racing livery with white top and red flanks. We pulled out of the defended gates of the station car park and took off at high speed in the direction of Omagh.

Within a quarter of a mile we hit a sleeping policeman in the road and the car went hurtling out of control and into a dry stone wall skirting the road side. From the moment that we hit the obstruction to reaching the wall everything seemed to go into slow motion and then nothing. Everything went blank.

I became aware of someone saying, "Oh, my fucking head," over and over again. As I listened to the voice I felt a total detachment from the situation. The voice seemed to go on for ages, the same four words repeated. 'Why,' I thought, 'does he keep repeating himself'? The voice was familiar to me, but I didn't know who it belonged to. As time went by and the voice droned on, I became aware that I was sitting in the road and there was a doctor attending me. I was holding my head with both hands and still saying, "Oh my fucking head." I don't know how long I had been unconscious, but it was long enough for help to have arrived at that very remote spot, and for the doctor to be sent for. The car was a total write-off but Dinger was okay. I was badly shaken and very confused. It was perhaps five or six more minutes before I felt for my personal weapon in its holster and found it was missing.

We searched the wreckage of the car, which was a total write off, for the pistol but to no avail. Then the road and its drainage ditch were investigated. It was half an hour later before I found the gun in a ditch about thirty yards from the wreckage of the car. I suppose I had Dinger to thank for pulling me from the wreckage of the Mini, but I didn't remember a thing after my head hit the windscreen.

We got a lift back to Omagh from one of the Land Rover drivers, and a couple of days later I went sick. My injuries from the crash kept me in our friendly little Medical Centre for ten days. During my stay I was jabbed and pulled about but enjoyed the best physical and mental relaxation that I had had for over a year.

The bomb in the Silver Birch Hotel turned out to be a small device that had been placed behind one of the radiators. It had done little harm, no one was injured and no real damage was done to the pub.

Our Medical Centre in camp was run by an army doctor and was staffed by a couple of local civilian nurses and two army medics. The centre was run like a small hospital and treatment was given to soldiers for minor medical ailments and injuries. The IRA had threatened to bomb NHS hospitals that treated military personnel, therefore for security reasons any treatment that soldiers required involving an overnight stay, had to take place in a military hospital or a Medical Centre. During my stay there were up to eight patients at any one time. The doctor was always on the lookout for combat stress, which was always a potential fact of life on long tours of active service, as well as the run of the mill ailments. I heard of some occasions when a soldier went sick with some miner ailment and was immediately hospitalised because the doctor recognised symptoms of stress. Our treatment from both doctor and staff was excellent.

The centre was located outside the camp perimeter and on one occasion I was visited by two very scruffy looking men; one had long greasy hair and several days' growth of beard. The other was middle aged with long grey hair and heavily worn working clothes. The civilian nurse who was on duty later commented on them, stating that she thought they were the IRA and that they had come to take me out. They were in fact, Bill from the grave yard op and another 4 Field Troop soldier. We often tasked them to do reconnaissance and surveillance operations; they thankfully didn't bring flowers or I would have wondered where they had got them from. 4 Field Troop were the forerunners of 14 Intelligence Company, a highly accomplished and somewhat notorious Special Forces unit, who at that time only operated in Ireland.

On one memorable occasion, a shiny new Rupert (officer) who had just completed his training at the Royal Military Academy at Sandhurst and had been placed with the Operations Officer at Lisanelly where it was hoped he could do no harm, asked a 4 Field Troop soldier who was hanging around the ops room waiting for Bill - who Bill was? The soldier who was dressed in the fashion of a tramp answered. "That's Bill." The frustrated young officer who thought he recognised a tone of insubordination in the man's reply, demanded, "What rank, is he?" to which he was answered. "Don't know mate, I think he might be a warrant officer, but who gives a fuck". When my time in the Medical Centre came to an end, I left strapped up with a bandaged and immobilised arm, but feeling rejuvenated.

Playing with Fire

The catalogue of misery continued throughout September with bombs in the Augher Creamery on the 19th of September and on the 20th the Carlton Hotel and Post Office in Belleek where two bombs went off within a few minutes of each other. The first and smaller bomb containing about fifty lb of explosives went off in the Post Office at about 9.30 AM. A couple of minutes later a much larger car bomb was detonated outside the Carlton Hotel. This explosion badly damaged a number of other buildings nearby but thanks to the prompt action of "C" Sqn Assault troop who were at the scene and quickly cleared the area before the larger device detonated, no one was killed.

This technique of placing two bombs with the larger one going off shortly after the smaller one was a classic way of achieving a large number of casualties. People trying to escape the area of the first bomb, which often came with a short warning, would be caught out by the second explosion. The worst case of this form of attack took place at

Warrenpoint on the 27th of August 1979 when a similar double bombing took the lives of 18 soldiers and seriously injured 6 more. This atrocity was the greatest loss in a single action that the army suffered during the whole of the campaign.
In the 1979 bombing, the deaths of 6 soldiers when the first bomb exploded brought a large number of other soldiers in response to it and it was these that were attacked by the second device, killing a further 12 with that explosion.

Facilities for off duty soldiers in the camp were pretty basic. There were the usual messes for officers and sergeants and a decent NAAFI which the other ranks went to in the evening, but one day in early 1974 we were surprised to see an enormous truck unloading what looked like rustic wooden beams and other building material. It soon became apparent that the beams were fake plastic replicas because of the way they were being manhandled off the wagon. They were in fact Fiberglas, but very realistic looking. A small work force next arrived and our interest became even keener when they started building what turned out to be a plastic replica of an old English pub. Both inside and out, it looked perfect and forty eight hours later it was complete. Thus the plastic pub was born.

I was walking back to the accommodation around dusk one evening when I noticed that the Int Cell and all of the camp lights had been turned on and there was a pleasant glow to the scene before my eyes. Some activity was detectable down past the plastic pub and towards the camp's main gate. The new guard were taking their turn to load weapons in the loading/unloading bay, in preparation for night duty. I turned away from the scene and went left into the Headquarters Building and climbed the stairs to the first floor.

The operations officer was briefing a couple of patrol commanders in the ops room, where one complete wall was covered with a large operational map of Fermanagh and Tyrone; lit up by spotlights from either side. In front of the map was a narrow stage area which stood about eighteen inches above the floor level of the rest of the room, in order that operational briefings could be given to up to thirty people at a time. I noted that the teleprinter in its glass walled room adjoining the ops room was clattering away. As I approached the Int Cell, Davy Steele, who was walking through the door, caught my arm.

"I was just coming to look for you, you need to go to the hospital and meet up with John Doherty.
He should be waiting for you in the car park, something to do with a firebombing."
The hospital was only about half a mile away from the camp so I walked there through the darkened streets. Detective Constable John Docherty was

sitting in his car when I arrived at the hospital. I didn't see him immediately, but he signalled me and climbed out of the vehicle when he saw me approaching.

 "I forgot to mention to Davy about bringing a camera, have you got one with you"? He enquired. "Yes. What's this about? All I was told was that it was something to do with a firebombing."
Doc went on to explain that two girls had been badly burned when they had tried to prime a fire bomb in the confines of a pub toilet cubicle. The resulting conflagration, enclosed as it was in the cubicle, had left them in a shocking state with extensive burns over much of their bodies. Photographs where needed for evidence, and as there wasn't a police photographer available, he was asking me to help. A look of concern must have found its way onto my face because Doc, who was a good friend, quickly assured me that Sinead was not amongst them. I was able to hear the agonised screams of one of the girls before we even arrived at the ward where they were isolated. Incredibly she was still showing a great deal of spirited defiance even though her legs, breasts and face had suffered deep burns into the flesh from the gas canister that had prematurely exploded.

The girls had tried priming their incendiary device ready to place it in a shop shortly before it closed for the night in order that the resulting blaze had plenty of time to get a hold before being detected. The incendiary device went off prematurely in the confined space of the toilet cubical where the two girls where crouched over it and now they were obviously in great agony. Yes, I felt sorry for them both, but if you play with fire there's every chance you will get your fingers burned.

On the 12th of October a particularly tragic event occurred when James McAdam, a young Catholic man, tried to help his elderly Protestant neighbour to escape when a bomb was thrown through her shop window. James was killed instantly when the bomb exploded, but the elderly woman, although badly injured, survived the attack. This young man's actions shone out like a beacon through the sectarian darkness of those dismal days. The light flickered, and then extinguished, when on the same day the Derg Arms which was situated on the main street of Castlederg, was yet again attacked by means of a car bomb, which was placed directly outside the busy pub. An alert police officer detected the smell of ANFO as he was walking past the pub and the whole area was cleared. The IRA phoned in a warning just three minutes before the device exploded. If it hadn't been for the fact that this 200lb bomb had been found earlier, the busy high street would have become a scene of carnage.

This was the second time within two months that the Derg Arms had been attacked in this manner. Most of the Bombs that the IRA manufactured constituted a quantity of ANFO which was made up from high nitrate fertiliser and diesel oil. To this main charge they would normally add a CO-OP primer made from animal feed sugar and diesel oil, which was activated by a commercial detonator. The detonator set off the CO-OP sometimes with the help of a commercial det cord (explosive cord, usually white) which in turn set off the ANFO. For a home cooked explosive it was incredibly reliable, but very smelly, which often gave its location away.

It says a lot for the tenacity of the locals that the pub was open again and doing good trade within a month. The IRA hadn't quite finished with Castlederg that week; three days after the pub bombing one was found in a Ministry of Agriculture digger on the outskirts of the village. It was a very busy time for me, especially as I had a special interest in the Castlederg area.

The Corgarys is an area of long valleys to the south west of Castlederg leading from county Tyrone through to the Republic. On the southern side of the border there was an enterprising Provisional active service unit. The village of Castlederg on the northern side was frequently attacked as was other nearby towns and villages. Usually these attacks originated in the Republic.

We had a great deal of intelligence about this ASU and knew most of its members. The way things worked were as follows: killings, shootings and bombing where the business of the ASU (active service unit), who were supported by other IRA members, who in turn were financed and encouraged by a substantial minority of the Catholic community. Everyone else stood by, unable through either fear or religious loyalty to do anything.

On the seventeenth of October the emphasis of our activities changed direction back to Fermanagh, when the village of Derrylin was attacked by a six man Active Service Unit of the IRA who had crossed the border from the Republic and struck the village. Using sub machine guns, they shot the post master Joseph Hall, and generally discharged their weapons in random fashion around the village. After only fifteen or twenty minutes they re-crossed the border into the Republic. As it was believed that they had planted a bomb before leaving, the ATO was sent for. I seem to remember the new ATO having to put RHQ straight about who was boss at the scene of a bomb.

When we received instructions from RHQ about the conduct of the bomb disposal operation, he gave them the one fingered salute and pointed out that even though he was only a staff sergeant it was he, not them, that was in command at the scene of a bomb incident. In the next two days we found a total of three devices in the village including one which was heavily booby trapped. The new ATO was quickly promoted to Warrant Officer by his unit (The Royal Ordinance Corps) in order to underline his authority. The nature of the booby trapping on the Derrylin bomb turned out to be one of the most sophisticated yet found.

During The Troubles, Derrylin had a disproportionate number of terrorist incidents for a village numbering less than three hundred souls.

'Doc'

My friend John Doherty had joined the metropolitan police and later transferred to the Royal Ulster Constabulary, and was now stationed in Omagh. Although Doc was ostensibly a CID officer he was mainly to be found working with Special Branch on anti-terrorist duties. Doc was a quiet man with a particular hatred for the Provo's, which for a Catholic born in the Republic, made him almost unique. This hatred definitely worked both ways; the IRA viewed Doc as a traitor and a collaborator and would do anything in their power to kill him.

We sometimes felt as if our hands were tied when dealing with the Provos. But Doc had a way of bypassing all the bullshit and getting down to the real nitty-gritty. This man broke the mould and therefore was a threat to the republican ego.
  John's family lived across the border in the Republic, in the Donegal village of Ballindrait which was only a short drive from his duty station in Omagh and he often went with his girlfriend to visit his mother on weekends when he was free of duties.

In mid October we received intelligence from sources in The Corgerys that the Provo's planned to whack Doc when he next visited his family in the Republic.

He was warned by telephone, but chose to ignore the warning. John insisted that he would take every precaution, by varying his time and route. He insisted that he knew what he was doing. John Doherty was one of the great heroes of the campaign; he died in his car near his mother's house in a hail of bullets when John Joe Jordan and Stan Corrigan ambushed him on the 28th of October 1973.
His girlfriend who was with him in the car survived the attack and came to my leaving party the following year. I wasn't able to bring myself to tell her about the great feeling of loss that I felt when Doc was murdered. I didn't know it at the time but I had had previous dealings with one of Doc's two killers. We had been approached a few months before the killing by Jordan, a Tyrone man from Dungannon who wanted to play the double game.

John's murder did Corrigan a lot of good in the republican movement. Within a few months, he would be organising the largest attack of the campaign at the Deanery in Clogher. When an ex IRA commander named John's killers to me, I was, to say the least, surprised. Neither Jordan nor Corrigan has ever been tried for Doc's murder.

I will always remember the interrogation of a known IRA man at the Police Station in Castlederg. We were getting nowhere with this man who was deeply involved with the Provo's. During a fag break Doc took his jacket off and put it on back to front. He then put his shoes on his hands and asked me to open the door to the interview room. To my amazement Doc did a handstand, and walked on his hands into the room. I closed the door after him blocking off the sound of surprised squealing, and things being thrown around. Later when I asked Doc about his strange behaviour, he answered that the man was due in front of a judge in the morning, and if he complained, do you think the judge would believe him when he described how he was questioned. Davy Steele another intelligence soldier who was with me at the time was highly amused by these tactics as indeed so was I.

On the way back to Omagh, Davy, who was driving at the time accidently discharged his weapon in the car missing his foot by about an inch and blowing a hole through the car's floor. Luckily the round ricocheted off the road, clear of the vehicle and didn't do any harm to the car's engine. The negligent discharge of a weapon was frowned upon by the army, for obvious reasons. So we covered up the incident and made up the shortfall of ammunition

213

later.

Who goes there?

We spent a lot of time moving around our two counties, setting up OP's in different locations, visiting police stations and patrol bases in order to glean bits of intelligence from patrol commanders and UDR soldiers alike, checking that the numerous border crossings that the IRA used for importing misery into the north were still impassable. There were days and nights spent lying in hides trying to catch shots with my camera, of some suspect or other, and whenever I worked in the Fermanagh region I would check in at the operations room in Angelo to let them know that I was in their area.

The road ahead of us shone wetly in the moonlight. There had been a slight drizzle of rain when we had set out from Omagh to check a few of the many illegal border crossing points around Fermanagh. Paddy Carrol was driving the old escort that the Army had repainted a garish red colour in a vain attempt to make it blend in with the dribble of other traffic on the roads. They often repainted so called covert vehicles, anything up to twice a year. After a while it was possible to tell them simply by the amount of paint they displayed. If this wasn't enough to give us away, one glance inside would confirm the onlooker's suspicions.

Army regulations stated that all vehicles were to carry a fire extinguisher between the driver's and passenger seats. Further confirmation of our military status would be instantly available from the fact that the extinguisher was furnished with olive green livery and covered in military markings. We simply covered the extinguisher with a coat or some material at hand but it was this kind of insane regulation that we found so frustrating. Someone, somewhere, a faceless military bureaucrat was still living in the 19th century and this added to the danger of our already precarious existence. The light was fading as we travelled back to Enniskillen having concluded our survey. I would describe our mood as pensive.

As we drove away from our last crossing point three shots had rang out in quick succession. The shots appeared to have come from the Republic which was 70 or so yards away to our right and were definitely fired in our direction. Though in theory we looked nothing at all like soldiers with our scruffy civilian clothing and long hair, the nature of our visit would have easily given us away. Paddy was still at the wheel and put his foot down and we speedily made distance away from the border. We both breathed a sigh of relief and we steadied our speed to make for our RV at the Enniskillen police barracks.

I don't know who noticed them first, maybe it was Paddy or maybe it was me. About quarter of a mile in front of us the road came to a crossing, and as it continued on the other side it disappeared into a patch of woodland. I counted eight plus men taking cover in the drainage ditch with the shade of the trees behind them. It was only possible to see them because of their moonlit reflections on the wet road. They were carrying weapons and some of them appeared to be wearing irregular camouflage clothing. We looked at each other furtively and Paddy slowed the car down. As we got closer they all dropped out of sight into what I supposed was a drainage ditch along the edge of the road. Not the usual tactics of an army patrol, I decided that these were either IRA setting up a VCP or British Special Forces (4 field troop).

In either case it was more prudent to keep the hell away from them, so Paddy executed a hand break turn in the middle of the road. At the point where we spun around we must have been less than a hundred yards from the junction and well within the range of their weapons. As we sped away and the echo of the screeching tyres died away, I became acutely aware of the vulnerability of my spine to the expected incoming gunfire. As our distance from the junction increased and my spine failed to disintegrate into a mess of soggy splinters from the expected hail of bullets, I began to relax. Some of the assault rifles that the IRA were employing at this time where powerful enough to easily pass through a car, including seats and occupants and our nerve-racking lives where such that we always expected the worst to happen.

The IRA was mounting numerous road blocks in the area at that time and it's possible that it might not have been one of theirs, but who would take that chance? Having already gone through the nightmare of being stopped by them in one of their vehicle check points I was happy to forgo that pleasure for a second time. A half hour later we were in Enniskillen police barracks drinking coffee. I can't remember us ever discussing this incident again, although the earlier shooting was registered as an incident.

A few days later I found myself in Enniskillen once more.

Enniskillen Rally

As our car sped its way through the folds of
darkness I could detect the glimmer of water to the
right of the unmade road that we were travelling
south on, behind which the vast emptiness of Lough
Erne spread its hidden blanket to the barely visible
horizon. The Q car that we were travelling in had
seen better days and was only held together with
the excessive amount of paint that the army kept
smothering it with. This and the constant change of
number plates were supposed to maintain the
vehicles invisibility when it came to the eyes of our
enemies.

 The cars windscreen was awash with the rain that
had accompanied us all the way from Omagh, but
this was now beginning to ease and our visibility of
the darkened landscape was starting to improve.
Davy Steel was driving, and seemed to have the
knack of finding every single bump and rut on what
wasn't really anything more than a track way
following the edge of the Lough. The car's heater
didn't work and the temperature inside had
plummeted because in order to keep the windscreen

clear of condensation, Davy left the driver's window partly open. To our left the shadows of the open fields and hedge rows of South Tyrone slid by and we would be shortly passing into the county of Fermanagh. The car was filled with an all invasive smell of dank countryside and exhaust fumes.

Our destination was to be a small air field about three miles to the north of Enniskillen called Saint Angelo. The First Tanks had a Squadron sized base there which it shared with the UDR and was used as a heliport for the southern part of our area. With the tour being such a long one many of the soldiers in the regiment had their families with them in Omagh. But only a small percentage of a soldier's time was normally spent in Tyrone's county town.

  Much of the rest of the time was taken up with manning the outstations or patrolling the countryside and villages of the border area. Often their families were left to fend for themselves with only a few off duty personnel to keep a watchful eye on their welfare. As two substantial bombs went off in married quarter's areas it would appear that the IRA viewed these families as their enemies, so those soldiers who were away from home for many weeks at a time must have felt a great concern for their welfare. Meanwhile their men where living for weeks on end under poor conditions at patrol bases like Saint Angelo, with hours, days and weeks of tense boredom often interceded by moments of stark terror when they came under attack.

Another fifteen minutes of driving on what had become a better paved road and we were within sight of the lights of Saint Angelo. The base consisted of a vast array of temporary portakabin style buildings laid out in a kind of grid structure. This strange looking mess of buildings was surrounded by a high steel wall topped in places with watch towers and configured as fortifications with the usual wire mesh and sand bags in profusion to defeat incoming fire.

At the main gate to the complex we showed our ID cards and were waved through to the parking area. I had only been to Saint Angelo a few times before and most of these visits had been made in daylight. Now in the darkness the whole edifice took on a different, more sinister aspect. It was about eleven at night, so the usual hustle and bustle of patrol change overs was taking place around us, but the other day to day activities had died down to a minimum. Everything was quiet, or at least as quiet as it can be in a village made from steel containers, sticky tape and wire mesh!

1 RTRs small operations room was brightly lit with the walls covered in maps and lists of operational patrols. A couple of desks lined one of the side walls of the room which appeared to be made from a couple of joined up steel cabins. It was the sort of

place that wouldn't look out of place as an architect's office on a building site. But this was no building site; the troops here were either out on patrol, or on twenty four hour standby, with just a few on their rest cycle.

The whole of this strange encampment was perched on the edge of an old airfield and looked like it was a bodge up of fortified accommodation, and a massive projection of British Army power on the outskirts of Enniskillen. After checking in with the ops officer, I went to find a bed for the night.

The next day I had a job to do, it was to be the day of the big republican march through the city and my task was to get as many photographs of leading republicans and upcoming stars as I could, without getting myself into trouble.

The march and rally was being held in Enniskillen in commemoration of the Derry marches which had taken place five years previously. Whenever one of these landmark events took place on either side of the political and religious divide they seemed to want to repeat it in order, I suppose, to gain the same result, i.e. bloodshed and chaos. But this kind of event was a godsend to us because instead of having to go looking for them individually, and in all kinds of difficult and often dangerous circumstances, we were able to find them all together in the same place. And an added bonus was the fact that the act of procession, of which they were so fond, meant they were all facing in the right direction for my camera. Of course the drawback was that to achieve my goal meant taking considerable risks by mixing in with a large crowd of republicans. Before the demo began I left my personal weapon and anything else that might give me away as a soldier in the RUC Barracks. A pistol is of little use when you are surrounded by hundreds of potential assailants. By carrying one you are simply offering them a means by which you might be quickly dispatched. I carried only my home made imitation Press Card, and one or two other carefully chosen items. There had been recent speculation in the papers and on national TV about the danger to legitimate newspaper people caused by undercover soldiers using faked press credentials. The way I viewed it, the IRA needed the press as much as the press needed them, and they were careful not to target press members, whereas I needed that cover to make things a little safer for myself. I quite fancied surviving my stint in Ireland and to get my photographs I needed to mingle with the crowds of supporters who were already lining the streets of the town and if noticed by the wrong people, I was dead meat.

To begin with things went very well. Part of the procession's route took it through an area of dingy streets of semi derelict houses. I found a viewpoint on a wall which enclosed the front steps of a house, from where I was able to get hundreds of close-up shots of the advancing procession. I had a battered old army Pentax camera around my neck and my fake press card which was made up from a piece of green card with Letraset adhered on to it, dangling from my neck on a long white cord. For all the effort that I had put into its manufacture it still looked like a green card with Letraset covered in fablon. At one point I recognised a man whose interrogation I had taken part in a few weeks before at Castlederg. I glued the camera to my face in order to cover it, the man failed to notice me and the incident passed without problems.

The procession of demonstrators finished up on a large piece of derelict ground, generally known as the car park, about three hundred yards from the police Barracks. About five hundred people gathered in a semi circle with their backs to the Police Barracks in order to listen to endless speeches and condemnations of everyone from the police and army, to opposing political movements. By the time that the speeches started, dusk was descending upon the gathering and I was trying to get my last few photographs of the speakers, when suddenly there was shouting amongst the gathered crowd.
At first I didn't realise what was happening. But as I moved away from the demonstration towards the

police barracks, stones started to hit the ground around me. It was time to take a powder.

At this point a group of demonstrators broke away from the crowd and started running in my direction. I couldn't escape towards the police station because the crowd were between me and it. So my only alternative was to head for the town and start running like hell. I could hear the hue and cry behind me as I ran down one street and then another. The realisation hit me that I didn't have a clue where I was going, and that maybe they did. I needed to go to ground quickly. The light was fading fast as I turned another corner and saw a partly open gate to my left; I forced my way in.

Behind the gate sacks full of rubbish were piled up to waist height and the place stank. The yard that I found myself in was about twelve foot square and had a door leading from it to a grey dingy building which I assumed was a house. There was a large piece of wood lying near by which I grabbed to use for my defence. Pressing myself against the wall at the side of the gate, I then had time to ponder on the wisdom of leaving my gun in the RUC barracks. What seemed like an age went by before the pounding of feet passed by. Then there was silence, no sound, no movement, just darkness. I stayed in my hide for about another half an hour before changing my appearance as much as I was able to and gingerly ventured out to view the empty street.

It took me another fifteen minutes to walk through the deserted town to the RUC Barracks. I passed a couple of groups of people who were probably walking away from the now finishing demonstration. My camera was wrapped in newspaper and stuck under my arm; they took little or no notice of me.

A few days later I picked up a republican newspaper from a street vendor, which gave an account of the 'Rally and March'. Apparently when they had gathered on a car park opposite the RUC Depot for speeches, an incident occurred where members of the crowd stoned a forces photographer. The parliamentary traitor, Frank McManus MP warned the crowd about futile stone throwing. No mention was made of the mob that spent much of the early evening searching Enniskillen's back streets for me. It went on to say that Mr Tom Flatley of the Fermanagh Civil Resistance Committee who had organised the march had dribbled on at length.

Then finally, Mr Aldan Corrigan of Dungannon told the crowd that there would never be peace in Ireland until the Union Jack stopped flying over the country. He went on to describe the army as the torturers of the Irish, and concluded by urging the crowd to keep the rebellion against the British rule of murder and injustice going.

The stark reality of my situation was brought into

focus five months later when, under very similar circumstances, an officer from 14 Intelligence Company was captured and executed by a republican mob whilst photographing a similar march in Londonderry. I can find very little detail from military sources about this incident, except that Captain Anthony Pollen, who the army describe as being from The Kings Own Scottish Borderers, was murdered by the republican mob during a civil rights march on the 24th of April 1974.

The IRA on the other hand, stated that Captain Pollen, who it is now generally accepted to have been working undercover as a member of the 14 intelligence company along with another soldier, was recognised whilst photographing the march. The other soldier managed to escape the mob by taking to his heels when they tried to catch him. His quick thinking probably saved the soldier's life, but Anthony Pollen was captured and killed.

The IRA claimed that he was not tortured before being executed. They described his treatment as an "interrogation," and his subsequent murder as an execution. Their statement completely fails to explain the battered state of this officer's body and the numerous indications on it of torture. I for one don't believe their statement, which they released after the killing. The IRA stated that he was known to them from previous encounters, but it's possible that it was solely the nature of his activities on the day of his death that gave him away to them. There were in fact other instances when soldiers were captured and killed whilst performing these very dangerous duties. Undercover soldiers had to be prepared to stand alone against these vicious killers.

Christmas is coming

November of 1973 started quietly apart from an operation on the 15th to block illegal border crossing points. Nothing much was happening, but then on the 22nd things started to pick up a bit with a bomb attack against RUC, 1RTR patrol near to the village of Carrickmore, a 500lb culvert mine detonated by command line exploded between the rear two vehicles of the patrol. The last vehicle in line was a Ferret Scout Car of 1 RTR commanded by Sergeant Chuck Westwood and driven by Trooper Hellier of C Squadron. Trooper Hellier had no chance of avoiding the ten foot deep crater that had been created by the explosion and was quickly joined in said crater by a Ford Escort which had been following closely behind. The attack caused injuries to four people, none of which were life threatening.

Most of the country roads in Ireland are under passed by substantial culverts, the point of which is to dissipate, the considerable rainfall that that land is blessed with. These culverts are often large enough for a man to crawl into and were used by the

IRA to place very large bombs, in order to attack security force patrols passing along the road above. It is enough to state that the effect of these mines can be devastating. One that I witnessed left a crater over 20 feet deep and almost 40ft across.

Similar events, where members of the public and their vehicles ended up in the craters made by exploding culvert mines, happened a lot during the tour. You would have thought that people would have realised the dangers and stayed well clear of military and police vehicles. But no, they still continued to tailgate these security force convoys and ended up sharing their unexpected fate.

Then on the 25th of November the emphasis changed once again to the county of Fermanagh.
It was a cold autumn morning when I found myself in this remote border village. Belleek by name and bleak by nature, it was the most westerly outpost of the British Army. There had been an incident earlier that morning, and I had tagged along with our new ATO to find out what had happened. The main street of Belleek slanted down towards the river Erne which constituted the border with the Republic.

There was a lot of activity with military vehicles rushing around and people talking in small groups. Further down the street a civilian car screeched to a halt and two men in smart civilian clothes climbed out carrying sub machine guns. I recognised them as being RUC officers and the occurrence passed unnoticed by others. Belleek RUC station was a heavily fortified patrol base for "A" Sqn 1RTR and a regular target for terrorists as they were able to attack from the Republic without ever crossing the border into the north.

We were taken to Daily Park housing estate which stood behind the RUC station, to check on the remnants of two Russian RPG7 Rockets that had missed their target at the patrol base and landed there during the attack. The RPGs were spent and of no further danger so we collected all the bits and headed back to the base, where I met Sgt Roger Litchfield, who, during the absence of his troop leader, was in command of the post. Rodge told me what had happened.

It had been another long cold night on guard for Trooper Brooks of 3 Troop who was on his last stag in the gun position that was located on the roof of the RUC Station when all hell broke loose. He started receiving heavy gunfire from the Republic side of the river. Brooks returned fire with his SMG and started shouting, "Stand to, stand to." Rodge Litchfield who was an experienced senior NCO immediately took control of the situation, and organised the defences.

The two Russian RPG rockets which were fired at

the gun positions on the roof of the station went high missing it completely and ended up in Daily Park, the housing estate situated directly behind. By this time most of Assault Troop who had been asleep in bed when the attack began were returning fire from their gun positions on the buildings ramparts. Notably, Trooper Barraclough who had been ripped from a deep sleep when the attack started and now was engaging the enemy wearing only his tin hat and underpants. More incoming RPGs hit the building but where mostly defeated by the covering of wire mesh which was there for that purpose.

2nd Lt Stephen Evans who had been on patrol during most of the previous night, remained in his room blissfully undisturbed by the activity around him until the general noise level of impacts on the building, as it received hit after hit from incoming rockets woke him just in time to see yet another rocket pass clear through the wall and exit his room through the closed door, leaving him startled in its wake and covering him in dust and debris. Had he been standing rather than reclining on his bed, when the rocket passed through the room, it would also have passed straight through him.

Meanwhile the fire fight was drawing to a close. Sgt Don Crassweller of 3 Troop had started returning heavy fire using the Browning machine gun that was normally deployed on the roof. Two of the assailants were thought to have been hit by "A" Sqn fire. One of whom was seen to crawl off as if injured. Another fell and didn't move. Patrols were dispatched from the Station in order to ascertain whether there were any casualties amongst the civilians in the surrounding houses, and to act as a cut off from the high ground to the north. As was the case in many of the attacks in the area at this time, it was thought that about six men were involved.

The IRA had long had a trench system, dug along the hillside on the Republic side of the river, in order to facilitate attacks such as this one against Belleek Police Station. These actions were carried out without intervention from the Garda or the Irish Army.

Later on the day of the 25th of November I drove back to Omagh to find that in my absence one of the main stores in the town had been destroyed in a fire. Incendiaries had been set in the store's stock during the previous day's trading. They were set to detonate during the night. It being Sunday, the fires wouldn't be noticed until the building was well alight. Three shops in the town in total were targeted. But due to a police alert, two of the incendiaries were found before they could cause too much damage.

A few days later the IRA made another furious attack this time against the RUC station at Belcoo.

Belcoo was also a patrol base for 1RTR and is also in the county of Fermanagh. The RUC station came under severe rifle, machine gun and rocket attack from multiple fire positions across the nearby border in the Republic. One young soldier's action during this attack won him the British Empire Medal for gallantry as the following citation notes.

Citation Trooper Derek Graham Wooley
10th December 1973 Action at Belcoo County Fermanagh
At 2035 hours 10th December, 1973 the RUC station at Belcoo, County Fermanagh came under rocket and small arms attack from terrorists in the Republic. Tpr Wooley a Ferret scout car driver was a member of the RTR detachment posted in the Station to reinforce the RUC guard. When the attack began Tpr. Wooley moved to his 'stand to' position in the gate Sanger and engaged a terrorist fire position on the border bridge leading to Blacklion. He quickly realised that fire was also being directed at the station from a second terrorist position to the south-east, and that none of the defenders was able to effectively fire on this position. On his own initiative, and ignoring the rocket blasts and considerable weight of small arms fire brought down on the station, he ran to his Ferret, drove it unaided to the side of the station, brought the Browning machine gun into action and engaged the flashes of fire from the terrorist position 300 metres away. Once his machine gun began to fire, the

accuracy of the terrorist fire quickly fell off and
shortly afterwards the terrorists broke off the
engagement. From subsequent debriefing of the RUC
staff of the station and the Guardia who examined the
terrorist fire position, it became clear that the fire
brought down by Tpr Wooley had been very accurate.
The area around the terrorist position was found to
be chipped and marked. His action undoubtedly
contributed to the terrorists breaking off their attack
and will do much to deter future attacks.

Déjà Vous

In the early evening one day in December I was sitting at my desk in the Into Cell evaluating the photographic records of known terrorists. I had come across a man I thought I recognised who was currently working on a building project near the camp Quartermasters store. I was convinced that I had recognised this man's face from amongst the hundreds of photographs in our files. I soon found the photo and yes, it was a good likeness, tomorrow I would cross-reference his name with the list of people not authorized to work in the camp vicinity.

The office was empty apart from me; the only sound was the hum of someone talking in the Operations Room next door. My thoughts turned once again to Sinead, what was I to do with this woman? There was little doubt in my mind that she was working for the opposition. I was sure that she and her friend, Angy, were gathering low grade intelligence about troop movements and possibly transporting weapons and explosives around the province. They may well have been involved in other more serious activities for all that I knew. The old saying came to mind that you keep your friends close and your enemies closer! I had certainly been doing that!

I got to my feet and looked out of the window across to where the noise of running feet and men shouting drifted on the night air. Something must have kicked off, I thought. The Bomb Squad office, a single story building directly opposite and below me was lit up, and there was movement of both men and vehicles. The Duty Officer stuck his head through the doorway and said, "There's a car bomb at Omagh Police station", and then disappeared. I took the stairs two at a time in an attempt to get aboard the moving Land Rovers before they managed to get to the Main Gate of the camp. My effort proved to be in vain and I ended up walking the quarter of a mile down Gortin Road towards the town's police station.

Soldiers and police officers where running about trying to evacuate people from the station, the telephone exchange and the nearby houses. The new corporal ATO, who I hadn't yet met, was standing next to one of our armoured patrol vehicles, hurriedly climbing into his special bomb protection suit and generally preparing himself to approach the small van which had been abandoned in front of the Station.

The driver of the van had been hijacked earlier by a

group of armed men, who, after loading the bomb in the back, told him to drive to Omagh Police Station and inform the officers inside of its arrival. This had happened about twenty minutes ago and now there were up to about thirty people running around trying to remove the last stragglers from the houses that were close by. Road blocks had been set up by "A" Squadron to stop the public getting near to the killing zone.

As I approached the scene there was a great puff of smoke and a blinding flash as the car exploded. My whole world turned to a slow motion swirl of vivid colour. Unable to breathe, I was overwhelmed by the profound knowledge that I had been far too close to it. I was aware of the blanket of razor sharp particles mixed with heavier debris that was heading towards me. At one and the same time a large piece of body work from the vehicle flew past my head and I was picked up by the blast and thrown to the ground where I was cascaded with the falling debris. I glanced across to where the new ATO was standing, and in time to see him trying to cram his body between the wheels of the armoured car in order to avoid the back axel of the destroyed vehicle that was now bouncing down the road in his direction at a terrifying speed. Miraculously the axel missed both vehicle and ATO and continued its journey uninterrupted until finally hitting a wall further up the road where it came to a rest. I wasn't aware of hearing the bomb explode; there was just a sickening, pulverised silence. Of the entire people still milling around in the kill zone, no one had more than minor cuts and scratches. It was 7pm and the bomb which was supposed to detonate at 7.20 had exploded 20 minutes early.

The ATO was within 2 minutes of approaching the vehicle and we all felt as if we had been let off very lightly. The Police Station was destroyed with most of its frontage having disappeared leaving a ragged gaping hole across its full facade and exposing its interior. Other buildings close by were also severely damaged. I didn't wait for the cleanup to start. I felt shocked and saddened. Maybe I should have helped but I just walked to one of the local pubs and sat staring at the wall for an hour, and then went back to camp.

The bomb that went off at 7pm that night at Omagh's Police station contained approximately 300 lb of homemade explosives that had been secreted in a van. It was driven to the front of the Police station and parked there by its owner who was under threat of execution if he didn't follow the terrorists' instructions. The bomb exploded about 40 minutes later destroying the building and seriously damaging several other buildings including the telephone exchange close by. Many of the officers of the Royal Ulster Constabulary and the soldiers of 'A' Squadron who were still clearing the area came close to getting caught up in this deadly blast.

Devastation caused by this device stretched for more than two hundred yards from its epicentre where little, if anything, remained of the van that the bomb had been placed in. On this occasion the destruction was made worse by the extra debris created when other parked vehicles added to the witches brew. The car with its bomb was parked up in close proximity to other vehicles which, instead of damping down the effect of the explosion, simply added more fragmentation material to its devastating effect.

Omagh's RUC Station was only a short distance from the camp, so I was in plenty of time to almost lose my head when a large section of ragged bodywork came skimming past it. By this point in the conflict I had become almost immune to any kind of incident; it was just another job, no feelings, just an overwhelming and profound sadness which was always with me and a strengthened resolve to continue the fight. When I left the scene of horror I felt certain that we must have taken casualties.

The next morning I discovered that the only serious injuries where suffered by an elderly woman who had refused to be evacuated from her home. It was often a problem for security forces trying to convince elderly people to abandon their homes during these incidents. Time and again they would not budge and a great deal of precious time was wasted in attempts to convince them.

Christmas day passed uneventfully but on Boxing Day, Brendan McCaul, the landlord of a pub in Clogher was confronted by two masked men who left a small suitcase in the passageway next to the bar. They told Brendan that the bomb would go off shortly. In fact it exploded within ten minutes, devastating the bar and barely giving Mr McCaul time to get people clear of the area. Interestingly this bombing, although unimportant in itself, was the beginning of an escalation of IRA interest in the Fermanagh village of Clogher, which would culminate four months later in the largest IRA attack of the whole 27 year campaign.

The 12th Jan turned out to be just another day at the office. At 7pm we received warning of a bomb in a van that was parked outside McGittigans pub on Campsie Road in Omagh. A Few minutes after our arrival at the scene and thankfully before ATO had a chance to inspect the Morris van that the bomb was positioned in, the bomb exploded. I was taken completely by surprise by the explosion which threw me several feet down the road and left me sitting there on my backside with metalwork flying all around me once again. Several of us were well within the blast radius, but no one was hit by the huge amount of flying metal and debris from the exploding vehicle. I did notice that afterwards there was a residual effect on my body from this incident; my breathing became quite laboured and difficult for several days. One of my mates suggested that maybe a lung had partially collapsed in the blast. In any event the effect was short lived and I had fully recovered within a few days.

The timing of the device was such, as to make me believe that this bomb was designed to kill our new ATO. These car bombs where an incredibly effective weapon in the hands of an unscrupulous terrorist. They were in fact like a one ton fragmentation grenade, except that they were easily moved around in order to place them for best effect. When one went off correctly, there was very little of the actual vehicle left intact; all of the bodywork, chassis, engine and axles would either disintegrate into fragmented flying debris or, in the case of some of the larger heavier parts, be thrown anything up to two hundred feet from the position that the intact car originally stood in. As you can imagine the cumulative potential for deaths and severe injuries from this mist of high speed particles and great lumps of metal was enormous.

When I met Sinead that evening, she was fascinated

by the array of bruises on me and unusually, commented on them. It was an unspoken rule that we never questioned each other about our day job or in fact anything else!

On the day after Boxing Day a Royal Engineers search team found a bomb near Kinewley which was disrupted by means of a controlled explosion. A small amount of the explosives were set off during the disruption but no major damage was done to the road or surrounding houses. It was believed that this device was laying in wait for a security forces patrol to stray over it, in order to kill its members. The bomb was the second largest to be found in the province at that time, the largest being Hoben and Sillery's bomb at Belleek which is also in County Fermanagh. Pressure of work in other areas made this the last major bomb incident that I was able to attend routinely for its complete duration. After the 27th of December I only attended bomb incidents if they fitted in with what I was doing.

Captain Cormack McCabe

A few days later, and still in early January, I found myself at a political meeting in the old Orange Hall in Omagh. The meeting was chaired by a leading member of the Orange Order and I found some of the language, to say the least, to be colourful. At the end of the meeting, during prayers, God was requested by one of the speakers to save us from the Papist Hoards. I took this to mean their Catholic neighbours. During the meeting the Reverend Ian Paisley, who was surrounded by some very tough looking men that looked to me like soldiers, spoke very informatively about the disappearance of a UDR Intelligence officer. As far as I knew, this event, which had happened the previous day, was being kept secret in order not to let the IRA know who they had got. He was very well informed about all the details of this abduction and was passing this secret information on to the hundred and fifty or so people in the hall.

The next day, which was a cold miserable day, I was called to the scene of a murder. A body had been found on the Ulster side of the border within a few yards of the Republic. I recognised the Special Branch officer who was in attendance as Detective Inspector Peter Flanagan, who was based in Omagh. We chatted for a while to give the army search team time to look for booby traps in the area of the body. When the search was complete we went to inspect the murder scene. The body itself, I was told, was of a man called McCabe. The moment we got close and I was able to see the body, I recognised him.

We had our suspicions who the body would belong to when we set out for the site of this atrocity, but the name didn't mean anything to me. It was a shock when I recognised him immediately; he was dressed in civilian clothing and was laid on his back, the obvious victim of an IRA execution.

Captain Cormack McCabe was the Intelligence Officer of the 4th Battalion the Ulster Defence Regiment, who I had heard Ian Paisley talking about, the day before. Captain McCabe was a regular visitor to our Operations Room and an occasional visitor to the intelligence cell. He had gone missing the previous day when he had taken his family to the Four Seasons Hotel in Monaghan, across the border in the Irish Republic, ostensibly for a family meal. We found out later that he was on an ill-conceived intelligence gathering expedition in the part of Monaghan known in military circles as, "The Enclave."

This area of the Republic was bordered on three sides by County Fermanagh in the north and west and county Armagh in the east, and was used by the IRA for a constant stream of cross border attacks. The pub restaurant was an infamous IRA haunt and republican meeting place. We could only surmise that Cormack was recognised by Provo's who were in there, and when he visited the toilet they took him prisoner. 43 year old Cormack was never seen alive by his family again. His captors tortured him and took him on foot a few yards across the border into Ulster before executing him. It was normal procedure for the IRA to do their killings in the north in order to give the impression that The Republic was peaceful.

It was thought that Cormack, who in his civilian life was a school headmaster, had been on these self-assigned intelligence gathering expeditions before the day of his capture. But on this occasion the courageous officer's luck ran out. According to a source within the IRA Cormack was tortured and executed by Brian Keenan and Morris Prendergast. It would be easy for us to criticise people like Cormack for taking un-necessary risks but when you're fighting a war with one hand tied behind your back the actions of brave individuals, commissioned and performed out of sight of authorities can be what sometimes make the difference.

Someone said, "Dave pull his arm across." so I pulled his arm across his body, only to find that it sprang back due to rigor mortis. I tried again and managed with difficulty to turn the rigid body over. We were now able to see the two bullet holes in the back of his head. Remarkably both his hands and the lengths of his arms were covered in blood. This disturbed me quite a bit because I figured that he was still alive after the shots were fired. There was no sign of an exit wound for either of the shots that had been fired into Cormack's head.

When the body was rolled someone noticed fragments of white detonator cord beneath it. The commonly used explosive cord was often used by the IRA as part of a primary detonator. There were also some clippings of electric cable. It was probable that those were the remnants' of some previous incident. But as we were so close to the border, and overlooked by hills in the Republic we decided to get a chopper in to scan the radio frequencies in case of radio controlled booby traps. As it would now be at least two hours before we were able to get back at the body, we retired to the local pub for lunch. There were three of us in the pub, Captain Mike Mullen, Military Intelligence Officer for "M" Division, Inspector Peter Flanagen, a Special Branch officer from Omagh and myself. Within the next year

247

the IRA would make attempts against all three of these men's lives. We had a very nice lunch followed by a couple of pints of beer and settled down in conversation to wait for the go ahead for our return to the body. Peter Flanagen was a Catholic and therefore high on the IRA's list of targets for assassination, he was deeply feared because of his reputation and viewed by republicans as a traitor.

We returned to the body and continued with our inspection of the scene where we rediscovered the two bullet holes in the back of the head with no exit wounds which indicated to us the use of a poor quality of the ammunition. One of the bullets however was lodged just beneath the skin of Cormack's face having gone completely through his brain but being depleted of momentum and unable to travel the remaining distance to exit his body. Inspector Flanagan commented, "Bad ammunition." Within months he would suffer the same fate.

In the years since I have often thought how remarkably callus and matter of fact we had all become about everything.

Playing the IRA at their own game

Throughout '73 and into '74 we were plagued by the activities of an IRA Active Service Unit that was involved in cross border attacks and bombings in the Castlederg area of county Tyrone. The leader of this unit was a man who we shall call Sean Cross. In the early days of the campaign, when Sean was living in Ulster, he had turned up at the local UDR barracks where he joined up. Sean's enthusiasm for soldiering only lasted until the first day that he was issued with a rifle. On that day he disappeared along with the aforementioned firearm to his new home which was a few yards on the southern side of the border.

Sean, as well as being a murderer and terrorist, was quite a successful business man, and in no time at all was importing tractors and agricultural machinery from behind the Iron Curtain. Although Sean's cross border terrorist activities were of a high profile and frequent nature, he must have had some very good friends within the Garda. He lived and worked quite openly with little obvious police interference in his activities.

During late '73 we started to gather indicators that Sean was importing other things along with his tractors. The strong suspicion being that some of these crates from Czechoslovakia contained Semtex (plastic explosive) and RPG7s (rocket propelled grenade launchers). As we became aware, the RPGs were very effective against both our armoured vehicles and the buildings that we used for our patrol bases. Whilst the Semtex could be used either on its own, as an effective high explosive, or as primary charge for trouble free detonation of ANFO and other low volatility homemade explosives.

There was a great deal of discussion about this man's activities. In both Army and Police circles, plots were laid to either capture or kill Sean. His unabated activities made nonsense of what little cross border security co-operation took place at that time. He was cocking a snook at us and so were the Garda. In nineteen seventy three seventy four, we were still listening to and reading about senior southern Irish politicians claiming Ulster as part of the Irish state. And it felt to us like we were shackled by the infamous yellow card which every soldier had to carry. This contained his orders for opening fire. These orders denied him virtually every right of self defence. Then there was the border itself, under no circumstances, not even to save your life, were you allowed to cross the border into the Republic. There was no right of hot pursuit if you were under attack from the Republic, you simply returned defensive fire and let them get away. On many occasions our mobile patrols were attacked from across the border. The Irish Republic was a safe haven for IRA terrorists to operate from.

Our main target in that area of the province was a volunteer called Seamus Harvey who was a prolific bomb layer. Seamus though, along with another volunteer had helpfully just killed himself whilst transporting a large bomb across the border, the likely target for this device was Castlederg. If we could have taken out Cross as well it might have been enough to give some respite to the sorely damaged villages in that area of Tyrone.

What I heard later was that a soldier and a police officer were discussing the Cross situation in the Silver Birch one night. The police officer suggested that it would be a good thing if someone was to take a little trip into the Republic and whack Cross as he went around doing his nightly lock up routine at the garage, the soldier agreed. The plot thickened when a few days later the conspirators met again and discussed the acquisition of a weapon with which to commit this foul deed. The search for a clean weapon was instigated, which the police officer was to take charge of.
Only later when the Police Officer admitted that the

251

weapon was to come from a source within a Protestant terror group, did the RC soldier pull out of the plot, and only then on the grounds that he would be leaving himself open to potential blackmail. Cross was gunned down at dusk a few weeks later. He wasn't killed, but his injuries were enough to put him out of the game. A week after the shooting, the soldier and the police officer met by accident and shared a taxi from Omagh to Lisanelly. "You did it then," said the soldier. "What?" replied the police officer with a guarded glance? Both of them knew exactly what the other was talking about, but there was a traditional game to be played.

The IRAF

Not everything that happened was as serious. The IRA managed to provide us with some light entertainment from time to time. For instance on the 23rd January '74, what we laughingly labelled the IRAF, was born. Eddie Gallager, who was a provisional commander along with his lover Bridget Rose Dugdale, the daughter of an ex British Army Brigadier, hijacked a helicopter in the Republic.

After loading the chopper with a milk churn full of homemade explosives and flying it to the Ulster town of Strabane, they attempted the aerial bombing of the local police station there. The attack was not altogether successful on account of their discovering that, after they had set the fuse, they were unable to get the milk churn through the door of the chopper. I can imagine the panic that ensued when they realised that their short timer was ticking away with their bomb resolutely refusing to exit the hovering aircraft. They had to disarm the bomb in flight and jettison the harmless device in a nearby field. Rose and Eddie went on to steal millions in an Art theft and all in all had successful careers as terrorists.

On the 28th of Jan a warning was received at Strabane police station that a car bomb was sitting outside Newtownstewart police station. Our ATO was tasked to check out the silver Ford Cortina that was parked directly in front of a 75 year old widow's house. It was well after 11pm on a very cold night that the evacuation of local residents started. I attended with ATO and got photographs of the 24 bags of explosives that where packed into the boot of the vehicle. ATO estimated the bomb to be 200lb. On the next day, the 29th my old stamping ground Castlederg was hit again. A Ford Cortina with its boot full of explosives was placed in front of the post office during the evening.
  No warning was received and if it wasn't for an observant 9 year old, a heavy loss of life may have resulted. The little girl, who reported the bomb in time to clear the area, was the daughter of the post master. The child reported the bomb at 9PM and it

exploded at 9-02PM. It was a close shave for everyone concerned. Many years later I was glancing through a book about the Army in Ireland and was surprised to find a photograph of me taken in Castlederg the following morning. I was viewing the scene of the devastation from this bomb.

This constant barrage of murderous attacks was enough to make anyone consider taking the law into their own hands. We knew that Castlederg's misery was mainly at the hands of one small IRA active service unit in the Republic, led by the owner of a garage there. The garage owner had now received his come-uppance and later someone accused me of the shooting. Although I knew more about it than I ever admitted, I was innocent of this attempted murder.

The long suffering town of Omagh once again had its turn in February. Between February the 4th and the 16th three major bomb attacks occurred which completely devastated the small market town. On Monday the 4th a hijacked post office van exploded on Market Street, the town's main thoroughfare, where 9 shops were wrecked and thirty other shops and pubs had their windows blown out. The action of the RUC and Army in clearing the area at no insignificant risk to their own lives stopped anyone being killed. Parts of the exploding vehicle where thrown up to 150 yards causing some injuries amongst members of the security forces who were still present at the scene.

Five days later on the 9th, while the clean up was still taking place, another large bomb attack took place. This time the target was the Crown Buildings, housing the government offices such as Social Security, Ministry of Agriculture etc. At the same time four of the remaining undamaged shops in the town were targeted by fire bombers and gutted. Then on February the 16th while the town was still reeling from these other attacks, another Post Office van which had previously been hijacked along with its driver, exploded leaving the town looking more like Stalingrad than the small county town that it was. The driver of the post office van, who had previously been forced to deliver a hijacked van, plus bomb, to 1 RTRs married quarters, must have started to feel victimised when he was once again hijacked. He was told by his tormenters that if he didn't deliver the bomb to Omagh centre they would blow him and the bomb up by remote control. Amazingly Omagh continued to function without the different elements of the community starting to tear each other's throats out, so if this was the effect the IRA had intended, it was a failure. I for one was amazed at the courage and fortitude shown by the people of that friendly little town.

Throughout March and April the litany of outrage

continued with murderous attacks taking place against the populous of first Tyrone and then Fermanagh and we were working hard to confront their vicious assaults. There was a kind of gray look to the soldiers of the First Royal Tank Regiment, many were getting close to the limits of their endurance, but they still soldiered on. I personally felt driven, whether it was by hatred or by something not yet defined, I didn't know. These comrades of mine had been working at ninety percent for over a year, and things where just about to get worse.

Things Get Worse

It all started on the 2nd of March with a car bomb in Castlederg. A grocery van was hijacked whilst doing deliveries at the unlikely named Laughtfoggy which is situated on the border with the Republic and lies only a few miles west of Castlederg. The 200 lb bomb was loaded into the van amongst the remaining groceries and the driver was told to drive it into Castlederg and abandon it there. In order to be sure of the driver's obedience, his assistant was held captive under threat of execution until the bomb had been delivered? The ATO was called and a tense eight hour vigil took place while he tried to make the device safe. Bombs that don't go off quickly are often booby trapped, so special care must be taken when handling them. Having lost one ATO to booby traps, we were keen not to let it happen again. Our ATO tried disrupting the bomb with two controlled explosions and an incendiary device, all of which failed and it exploded while still being worked on, eight hours after being planted, causing a great deal of damage and further wrecking many buildings which were still being repaired after previous attacks. Luckily the ATO was on a break away from the bomb when it went off.

Five days later on the 7th of March a hijacking and bombing took place, this time on the outskirts of the town. An 11 year old boy and another occupant of a car were held hostage by the terrorists, while the driver was made to deliver a small bomb to a service station. The bomb did little harm and the whole exercise seemed pretty pointless. A number of children who were in the area returning home from school, where shocked and frightened by the explosion of the device, but other than this it was a pathetic wet squid.

Just over a week after, on the 15th of March, a police land-rover patrol from the RUC barracks in Castlederg was ambushed by an IRA active service unit near the border. The two young police officers in the Land-Rover where fired upon by men using assault rifles and returned fire with their Sterling sub machine guns. The officers were badly outgunned by the superior fire power, accuracy and range of the IRA weapons and had to go to ground. The Sterling Sub Machine Gun was a poor weapon with little power and range and as now been replaced by better suited weapons. It does not stand up well against an assault rifle at any range and the army where glad to see the back of it. The officers where outgunned and outnumbered by the terrorists, nevertheless the gun battle continued for over twenty minutes before the army and police heard anything about it. Twenty five minutes after the first shots were fired the cavalry arrived in the form of the police desk sergeant from Castlederg and two constables who where all armed with assault rifles. The increased firepower soon sent the gang scuttling back across the border into the safe haven of the Republic.

The next act in this brutal display took place ten miles to the east of Castlederg in the small township of Newtownstewart, where, eleven days later on 26th of March, two men were reported to have abandoned a Transit van outside the cash and carry on Strabane Road. The 300lb bomb caused moderate damage to the town.

With all this activity occurring around the western border of Tyrone with Donegal the IRA had not forgotten Omagh. On March the 23rd a retired army major who worked in the Army Careers Office in the town was murdered in a drive by shooting. Fifty year old Major Donald Farrell was taking his dog to an area on the outskirts of Omagh, where he normally walked the animal. The van that he was driving was riddled with bullets in the attack and both Major Farrell and his dog were hit several times and killed. It later transpired that the intended target was in fact Mike Mullen.

April 1974 shaped up in a similar manner. On the 7th of the month a Saracen armoured car of 'C' Squadron was blown up by a large culvert mine in the Castlederg area, both the driver and commander sustained minor injuries. The mine left a crater 10 ft deep by 20 ft in diameter. Across the border in the Republic and about 250 yards away, three men were seen running away from the scene. The bloodied crew of the Saracen briefly engaged the fleeing assailants with rifle and machine gun fire, but Garda officers who arrived on the scene reported that there were no casualties found on the Republic side of the border.

Then on April 12th the actions of an observant patrol commander brought about the capture of a substantial amount of weapons and explosives when he saw a fertiliser bag being blown about in a field. The bag contained a detonator and other bomb making ingredients. A further search by members of 'B' Sqn and soldiers of 6 UDR, who were called in to help, uncovered a substantial amount of bomb making equipment, explosives, weapons and ammunition.

The IRA's Big Push

Just nine days later, a Saturday night drinking session turned into a nightmare for one man who came staggering out of the pub around midnight He was just in time to catch the full blast of a car bomb which had been placed on the main street of Newtownbutler. A police officer who was attempting to clear the area at the time was also severely injured in the attack. Both men lost legs in the blast and were very lucky to escape with their lives. The car bomb which exploded early on April 21st was huge, containing as much as 800lb of explosives. There was a vast amount of damage done by both the explosion and the large amount of flying debris, to both the shops and houses in the town centre.

The car had been hijacked earlier, near Clones on the Fermanagh side of the border, after loading the vehicle with the bomb, the armed gang of hijackers kept the passenger as a hostage and instructed the driver to take his vehicle into Newtownbutler and abandon it on the main street. He was told that any deviation from his instructions would result in the passenger being killed. To his credit, on leaving the car on the main street the driver ran around shouting warnings and helped clear the area.

Newtownbutler in county Fermanagh is hardly more than a village and is the most southerly place of note in Ulster. Its position next to the Monaghan Enclave made it very vulnerable to this form of attack. A little further north and about fifteen miles from the border with the Republic, lay the village of Clogher, this was to be the IRA's next target. This short period of activity culminated on May 2nd 1974 with the largest attack of the entire campaign, against the old Deanery at Clogher.

During the days leading up to the 2nd of May reports started to come in about potential IRA activity in the border area around the village of Clogher. One such report was of a group of men standing around a car examining maps. One of the men was recognised by our informant as a local provisional commander who was very active in the area. The old Deanery in Clogher which had fallen out of use many years before and had been purchased by the army and was now the headquarters for a company of the 6th Battalion of the Ulster Defence Regiment and was used by 1RTR as a patrol base. Like most military buildings in the province, the Deanery was heavily fortified and was covered with steel mesh in order to defend against mortar and rocket attack. The idea being that any rockets or mortar shells fired at the building would first hit the steel mesh covering which it was completely cocooned in and explode harmlessly against it; rather than punching a hole through the exterior walls and exploding in the building's interior. Windows were bricked up and doorways defended. The building was situated on the outskirts of the village and was partly surrounded by farmland.

As the days went by, we became aware that something big was building up. It was no coincidence that the Intelligence Cell in Omagh was fully manned during the night as the first reports started to come in.

Then shortly before midnight on the 2nd of May it all blew off. At first, reports started to trickle in that there were a number of IRA road blocks springing up on country lanes, in the area around Clogher. The Provisionals were trying to isolate Clogher and we smelt a giant rat. Because of all the small indicators that we had been receiving, we had been focusing more on Clogher for a couple of weeks, so the reaction was instantaneous. Captain Chris Holtom, who was our Intelligence Officer, ordered all Intelligence assets into the area to find out what was going on. Within minutes of us starting out for

Clogher, to what was possibly the largest attack in the history of the Provisional IRA, the Deanery came under serious attack. If you include the volunteers manning VCPs and covering escape routes, there were between fifty and sixty volunteers involved.

Inside the Deanery the first they knew about the attack was when a rocket propelled grenade hit the building. This was swiftly followed by machine-gun and rifle fire. Fire was returned by the UDR and 3 troop of "A" Sqn 1RTR led by 2nd Lt Evans, who you will remember from his close shave with an RPG 7 rocket during the IRA's attack on Belleek Police Station, on this occasion Mr Evans was wide awake. 3 Troop had just arrived back from a Patrol. They mounted their scout cars and took up positions on the roads to the side of, and behind the Deanery, where they suppressed the enemy gun fire with their machine guns. The battle raged for some time with the building taking a lot of direct hits from Rocket Propelled Grenades and near misses from the fifteen plus mortar bombs which were fired, as well has a great deal of machine gun and rifle fire.

The amount of outgoing fire from 3 Troop eventually pushed the IRA out of their positions that they had taken along the side of a sunken road about two hundred yards away from the rear of the Deanery. Inside the building things hadn't gone so well. One UDR officer was seriously injured and needed casualty evacuation by chopper. During the worst part of the attack a 28 year old off duty UDR woman was killed when a rocket penetrated the wall of the staircase where she was sheltering with her husband. The rocket hit Private Eve Martin in her head. It took this beautiful young woman's life instantly. Under normal circumstances the Deanery would only have had a small number of soldiers operating the radios and the others would have been on rest breaks during the time of the attack, but luckily on that night a 1 RTR scout car patrol had just arrived back for a breather, so the incumbents where able to put up a vigorous defence and quickly take the offensive.

I spent the whole night moving around the area with Chris Holtom and four other members of our intelligence cell. We were building up a picture of the night's events. It appeared that the attack had started the previous day when the IRA had taken over a farm on the sunken road behind the Deanery. According to the farmer, he and his family were held prisoners until after the attackers retreated from their fire positions the following day. I personally found this difficult to believe. The farmer was known to me as a staunch republican with strong family links to the Provisionals. His farm had been a guesthouse to a number of volunteers, and a vast amount of weapons and ammunition, for the period of up to eighteen hours.

When I questioned the farmer about his ordeal he became extremely aggressive and refused to answer any questions about the incident, furthermore he started to act in a paranoid fashion. I was, according to him, recording our conversation on some kind of bugging device. This was nonsense, the army didn't have the resources available to supply such hi tech gadgetry to the likes of me.

The main force of volunteers had crossed the border on foot and walked in. Later, after the attack was repulsed, a number of volunteers in a large van were engaged by a UDR patrol whilst trying to affect an escape across the border into the Republic. The volunteers who were in what was described as a removals van, opened fire, and made a run for it. They were seen heading for a house on the southern side of the border which belonged to the cousin of our unhelpful Farmer. The cousin was also a, "staunch republican." I believed that both men were fully engaged in this murderous attack.

Sinead to Nottingham

At the beginning of March Sinead met me in the pub on a mid week evening. I was surprised because she would normally have been working at her night shift in the hospital.

"I've been trying to find you for two days," she said accusingly.

"Why, what's the matter," I asked.

"The day before yesterday I was called in to Omagh police station to see Flanagan, who told me that I had to leave Ulster within four days or he will find something to charge me with."

"He's bluffing," I said. "There is nothing for him to charge you with - is there?"

"I can't take that chance," she retorted, ignoring my question. "I'm going to have to go and stay with my brother in Nottingham for a while."

Apparently DI Flanagan thought he was the marshal in a bad cowboy movie. It crossed my mind though that he may have been looking after my interests in a funny kind of way. He may well have thought that every moment I spent with her; that I was in great danger of being targeted by her friends. In any case I was quite relieved that she was to be extracted from this mire, if only to keep her out of trouble. I had a course coming up in Aldershot and hopefully some leave afterwards. I would visit my mother in Oldham and spend the remainder of my leave in Nottingham with Sinead. It would be a strange feeling to meet without the chance of dangerous situations arising. I had never visited Nottingham, and was quite looking forward to it. This beautiful woman would leave a vast hole in my life; I would miss her like hell, but recognized that she would be in a better place.

Sinead's nemesis, Inspector Peter Flanagan was one of the few Roman Catholic Special Branch officers in The RUC at that time. His family background and religion put him right at the heart of the extremist politics that motivated the republican movement in Ireland. He sat like a sinister spider at the centre of a complex web of intrigue. His reputation, which he made little attempt to change, was one of an astute controlling hard man. As with all Catholic police officers he was viewed as a traitor amongst republicans. And he was high on the IRA's list of potential assassination victims. None of this stopped Flanagan from doing one hell of a job. Most evenings would find him sat at the end of the bar in Brodricks Bar which was situated next to the court house, the old site of O'Neill castle, in Omagh. Month in and month out he sat there, a powerful presence in this Catholic pub, as if tempting the IRA to do something about it. Later in that year, they did do: Peter Flanagan constituted a major player in that Soul-less Labyrinth of deceit and treachery that we played.

Within two days Sinead had booked a ferry crossing for her and her little Mini Clubman and was gone. She was right to take Flanagan seriously. You didn't fuck with people like him.

Married Quarters Bombing

A week later, on Thursday May 9th 1974 the regiment's married quarters were attacked for the second time when a 200 lb car bomb was detonated in front of the Army Careers office in Omagh. This building stood near to St Lucia UDR Barracks and amongst the 1RTRs married quarters. The attack took place at around midnight and if the bomb had not been discovered by two UDR soldiers, the three minute warning that was given by the IRA would have just been enough to make certain that fleeing families would have been scythed down in the open by this murderous weapon. The car used in the attack had been stolen in Carrickmore. About thirty of the regiments' married quarters suffered damage, and the careers office was virtually destroyed by flying debris from the exploding vehicle.

The Plan

Early in 1974 I was given some leave in England. I was ready for a break and decided to visit my elderly mother in Oldham. It was there that I met up with Alpha. Although it complicates my story somewhat, I have promised this important character his anonymity and even though it means holding back many of this brave man's actions, I am determined to fulfil his wishes. I may therefore seem a little vague as too much detail may give away his identity.

Having just spent a couple of days relaxing in my mother's small flat, I decided to go to the pub for a drink. The nearest pub to her house on Saint Mary's estate was a pub called the Centurion, which at that time, was quite new. The pub stood close to Oldham outdoor market, where much of its trade came from.

I entered the pub and chose a bar stool that gave me a good tally of the people who were entering and leaving the pub through the large back bar mirror. It wasn't long before a man of small stature, lean and

271

hard looking, walked in. All my defensive instincts told me that this was the man to watch. After finishing my drink I ordered another and he came over and bought his third pint.

His accent was a kind of mid Atlantic with a Lancashire twang to it.

A kind of recognition process was taking place between us, which developed into a suspicious standoff. He looked nothing like a soldier and neither did I for that matter, as both of us were sporting long hair, and in my case, several days of unshaven stubble. Alpha was the first to break the ice when he walked up and said, "Are you a soldier?" I was totally amazed, how the hell did he work that one out!! Without waiting for an answer he continued. "I just got out of the army last year." It turned out that he was a Royal Engineer who had finished off his last few years of his service with another unit which must remain nameless. But he was very-much involved with the army's undercover operations. Although no longer a soldier, my new friend was in need of some action. So after giving it a lot of thought I suggested that instead of going off to sell his soldiering skills abroad, he should join up with mc in a new venture that I had in mind.

I had already decided to leave the army and return to Ireland as a freelance intelligence gatherer. I didn't want to be too reliant on Peter Flanagan or anyone else. It was important to me that I was in control. Yes, it was true that in order to be financially and logistically viable I would be reliant on Flanagan and for him to keep coming up with the goods we would need to supply him with intelligence that was both relevant and useful. From my discussions with Mike Mullen I understood that as a civy I would become deniable and that made me very useful on politically sensitive operations such as surveillance across the border in the Irish Republic. If we were caught or killed there would be no comebacks for the British Government. I would be working mainly in the counties Donegal and Monahan from where most of the attacks against Tyrone, Fermanagh and South Armagh came from. What I needed was a centre of operations in which we would not stand out too much as strangers. The little seaside town of Bundoran in the republic fitted the bill. I needed to check it out.

Bundoran is situated on the west coast of Ireland, only a few short miles west of Belleek in County Fermanagh. The county of Donegal in which it is located butts up against Ulster and Bundoran is only a very short journey of 8 miles from the border with Northern Ireland. It was a pleasant run but parts of the route where sometimes open to the full force of the Atlantic's fury. This little town in the early 1970s had taken on the role of a kind of rest and recuperation centre for IRA volunteers between operations and the general republican masses sheltering from the conflict in the north. It would be the ideal place to act as the centre for our collection of intelligence on the IRA's activities. As a serving soldier, apart from the normal and obvious risks, your capture was likely to cause an international incident. I personally had little respect for the sovereignty of the Irish Republic, in line with their lack of respect for the UKs sovereignty. Others felt differently.

The thinly populated county of Donegal in the extreme north of the Republic is almost cut off from the rest of the country by Ulster's county Fermanagh; a searching finger of which points out across the conjoining landmass leaving only an 8 mile gap linking Donegal with the remainder of Southern Ireland. Donegal was second to county Mohnaghen for being the springboard for cross border attacks and many of those were aimed at Belleek and the surrounding towns and villages. Further north, the small towns of Castlederg and Stranbane were also high on the list of IRA cross border targets. So, within a few miles of those targets and bracing the Atlantic coast nestled Ireland's fun capital, Bundoran, and for someone like me it was far too much of a temptation to be ignored. There were lots of bars and fine hotels that catered for the holiday makers. The sea front was dominated by the massive, opulent Great Northern Hotel, overlooking the bay from its cliff top location. Everywhere one went there was the incongruous blare of American country and western music and occasionally, depending on the bar, relieved by the addition of Irish rebel songs. A kind of Wild West, frontier atmosphere prevailed. Surely this would be the place to blend in amongst the tourist while gathering intelligence in the surrounding border areas. This would be our base.

The financial rewards meant nothing to me. My motivation was to win this bloody campaign against the IRA. So, after we had got to know each other a bit better I put it to Alpha that he should join me there. He agreed. We now had a team.

Together with my new mate, I started to do some planning. Acquiring the weapons we would need was to be left to him. He had some good contacts in that field. My job was to arrange control and contact facilities. The acquisition of Alpha as an accomplice in this endeavour made the whole scheme much more realistically survivable. Money would not be a problem; the security forces operated a sliding scale of payments for undercover operatives for the gathering of intelligence. Starting at upwards of £30,000 for the capture or killing of a member of the IRA's Army Council, going down to subsistence payments for standby. The work was incredibly dangerous and had a low survival expectation but it was big money for the early seventies. A few months and then a move was the best we might expect. With Alpha on side though, I might be able to achieve something worthwhile.

It turned out that we were both once students at the same local Catholic school, St Mary in Oldham. My new partner, who was now working as a builder on the site of a new swimming baths, was about two years older than me, but in many ways we were like peas in a pod. Alpha was a bit eccentric and certainly drank like a fish but I felt instantly that I was able to trust him.

I spent three days in Oldham before going back to Ireland, by the end of which time; I classed Alpha as my best friend.

I knew that Alpha was chafing at the bit to get started. I figured that his soul had been damaged by years of fighting and without the close proximity of danger he didn't feel alive. But he was just going to have to wait.

The plan now was for me to finish my service with the army and allow a few months to pass in order to draw a definite line underneath my military service, and after that we would get stuck into the IRA and do the most damage that was possible. On a personal level I was totally committed to the fight and never even considered the ambiguity of my allegiance to my country and my love for Sinead, the decisions were made, it never crossed my mind that fate would intervene to scupper our plans.

I spent my last weekend before returning across the water in Nottingham with Sinead. She was staying with her brother on a council estate to the north of the city, and close to the City Hospital where I believe she was working as a bank nurse. My feelings for her where so powerful that I could have cut them with a knife and even drowned in them, for me it was not a comfortable or pleasant feeling. Although I wanted to be close and near to her all the time, I was glad to be going back to Ireland and away from her.

It was Nottingham to Liverpool by coach, then an uncomfortable ferry crossing to Belfast which always seemed to take weeks. Once in Belfast a bus to Omagh completed the journey.

The Old Comrade

On returning to Omagh from my leave I discovered that a new commanding officer had arrived in station. Lieutenant Colonel Walker was an officer of the highest quality and from the very start commanded respect from his hard pressed men. The command that he was to oversee covered the equivalent of 53% of the border with the Republic and at that time the most active in terms of large scale attacks in all of Ulster. His officers and men had almost a year's experience in the job under their belts, but there was a kind of fatigue setting in.

Some of the shocking events of that last year, along with the long dangerous hours that they had to work, were combining to have a negative effect on the troops. Lieutenant Colonel Walker was like a fresh breeze that affected all of our thinking. This man was special, the job in hand was the most important thing in the world for him, but trailing only a short distance behind that, was his genuine concern and commitment to the welfare of his men. You knew with this officer that if things went wrong

he would stand by you, a staunch ally. Lieutenant Colonel Walker was a soldier's soldier.
One morning in early May he called me into his office and explained to me a little quandary that had been playing his mind. He had been contacted by an ex soldier, who had been a member of his troop when he was a young subaltern.

The old comrade, who was now living in Omagh, wanted the colonel to meet him, saying that he had some information that should prove useful to the army in its pursuit of the terrorists. This was excellent news, these where exactly the kind of contacts that we were constantly trying to recruit. The problem though was that this man insisted on setting the venue for their meeting.
  What did I think? I thought, "No way." As far as I was concerned that must not happen. If this should prove to be a trap, we needed to be in control of the ground where the meeting was to take place. "Well," said the colonel. "I've already made arrangements to meet him in a pub at the side of the court house in Omagh." There was a short pause, and then he added, "In about an hour." I thought, shit! The Colonel must have been aware that he constituted a high level target for the IRA, but seemed unfazed by the obvious risk that he was about to take meeting up with this old comrade. He seemed to carry a strong emotional bond with the regiment and all of the family of men both serving and retired.

"Sir, I think I should check the place out first, before you go in," I ventured, "and then I can guard the door from the outside while you talk to him"
He agreed.

"And sir, can you try to get him to leave you out of the loop in future, we need him to be talking directly to us." He just nodded, which didn't fill me with confidence that he had taken my request seriously. Brodricks Bar was near empty, just a couple of old grizzled veterans keeping the bar in place. There was no sign of the man who was supposed to be there for the meeting. The atmosphere in the pub was sullen and gray, as the incumbents closely watched my approach to the bar and whatever conversation had been taking place came to an abrupt conclusion.

There was no one behind the bar, so I found a stool from where I was able to see both the door and the other customers, and waited. It wasn't long before a tubby little middle-aged woman appeared from a back room to serve me with a drink, and slowly the melodic hum of whispered conversation started up again.

This was starting to look like a no show. After half an hour or so I gave up and left the bar to meet up with the Colonel on the high street as we had arranged. As I approached him he looked for the entire world like a country gentlemen in town for the horse sales. It was two days later that the CO stuck his head through the intelligence cell doorway and indicated with the wave of a finger for me to go to his office.

"Do you have much on today?" he asked,
"Nothing I can't put off, sir," I replied.
"I've been back in touch and made arrangements for you to meet him in his house," he stated, meaning the old comrade. "He still wants to give the information to me personally but he's agreed to let you meet up with him first." He then proceeded to give me an address in Omagh and an approximate time to meet. In my head I thought. "Fuck that, I'll turn up in my own time." I was uncomfortable about letting this old comrade dictate timings and venues. I couldn't change the venue so I'd just turn up there early instead.

I didn't like the idea of this unknown entity calling all the shots and us trailing along carrying out his wishes. If I had learned one thing in the last year, it was not to trust anyone until they had proved themselves to me personally.

The meeting went off OK and when I returned to camp I found the Colonel still working in his office. "How did it go then?" he asked.
"Can I put this to you straight Sir?"
He looked irritated, "No need to pussy around, just say what you think," he commanded.

281

"Don't touch it with a fucking barge pole," I said. He looked up sternly from his desk and showed me the palm of his right hand in invitation to continue.

"When I arrived at the house, which was situated in the centre of a rundown Catholic estate, I was met at the front door by a sullen looking Irish woman who invited me in. There were a couple of other women present throughout my visit which lasted about an hour. Your ex Tanky was sitting in the living room sucking on a tube of local brew and looking the worse for wear. Empty beer cans were strewn about the coffee table and on the floor around him. This was at 3pm."

"Were you able to talk to him?" the CO interjected.

"Only about general things, there were too many people floating around and he seemed to be oblivious to them. His wallet was on the table in front of him," I continued, "and it was bulging with high denomination Irish bank notes, the weight of which was forcing the wallet open. The room was drab and tatty, smelt of neglect and there was a distinct lack of any indication that money had been spent on the upkeep of that house for many years."

"When he saw me looking at the wallet, he moved it from view so I commented on the money, asking where he obtained thousands of pounds in Punts from. After an extended thinking time he offered that it was the proceeds of a racing win in the Republic, and he didn't question my judgment that the loot was in the thousands. Meanwhile I was under the constant gaze of the Irish women in the room."

Lieutenant Colonel Walker glanced at is hands resting on the desk for a long moment, then looking me in the eye said, "OK then, what are your concerns with this?"
"Sir, there was nothing that I saw or heard that convinced me that there was even the slightest possibility that this man was going to give us anything but trouble. He appeared to have no sense of security and his home seems to be used as a drop-in centre for the estate. In fact my gut instinct is that you are being set up for a kill, not by him but more probably by someone using him."

Our meeting was at an end but as I was leaving the room he said, "I'll tell you one thing though, I'm minded to go through with this, so get your thinking cap on."
I needed to get my thoughts in order, it was flattering that this important man was laying such trust in my opinions, but I felt with a passion that he was right to do so. I lived and breathed this stuff and had become very good at it.

As I left and sauntered through RHQ towards the Intelligence Cell and on reaching the Operations Room I was confronted by an angry looking Major who was the OC of one of the sabre squadrons.

"What the fuck happened last night then?" he demanded angrily. I just looked at him with a perplexed and uncomprehending look on my face. "You told them to let her go," he gasped, in a tone of disbelief.

The previous night I had decided to go to bed early and try to get some sleep, there were local elections taking place the next day and it might get quite lively so I took the opportunity to chill out in my room which I shared with the Bomb Squad. At about 10pm the door burst open and the duty clerk from RHQ came in, and on seeing me he said accusingly, "Thank fuck for that, I've been looking for you everywhere, you're needed in Omagh." In response to my questioning look, he added, "All I know is that they are holding some women and want to know whether they can arrest her."

My first thought was it can't be Sinead, thank God, she's in England. I walked down to the location of the patrol that had made the stop. On approaching them I noticed two uncomfortable looking RUC officers to one side of the group. A small crowd of onlookers was beginning to gather and the police were expecting trouble. The Army patrol which was led by a young officer, were holding a woman and a man under special powers. They had had them detained for an hour which left another three hours before they had to be charged or released.

 Thinking that I recognised the female prisoner, I

got the patrol sergeant on one side and asked for her name. "She's Patricia Kelly," he said. "Do you know her?"

"I know of her," I said. "She's more of a political activist with a personal grudge against the army; courtesy of some solder who humped then dumped her." At this point the officer joined us. "She has got a bag full of seditious material," he said. I requested to look at these leaflets and posters that she was carrying, and he was right, it was very bitter stuff that she was peddling.

There was little if any truth in any of it and you could have made a case for incitement to murder from some of this material if you had found it in any other part of UK. "What do you think?" said the officer. "Can we arrest her?"

"I see stuff like that every day, they call it election material over here," I replied. "She's got close links with paramilitary's but she's not important and if I were you, I'd let her go, before you have a riot on your hands. We can grab her any time." The officer insisted that I first of all questioned her, which I did. She confirmed that the garbage that she was carrying was in preparation for the next day's elections and that she was a candidate. Both her and her election manager where duly released.

The still angry looking Major was less than impressed by my reasoning, and stalked off

285

muttering, "Fucking interfering bastards," over his shoulder and duly disappeared through the doorway towards the offices.

In a funny sort of way his manner and actions towards me where quite reassuring, it was as if the earth had turned upside down and the meek had just inherited it. Even though he thought that I had instructed his patrol commander, who vastly outranked me. It wasn't this insubordinate act that was bothering him, but rather the content of my alleged instruction which stuck in his military gullet. Oddly, he didn't question my right to do it. Funny old day that one!

Against my better judgment the day of the meeting arrived. The colonel was to drive his car to the car park of the Knock-na-moe Castle Hotel where only a year before five of our soldiers had been murdered. There was something that didn't ring true about much of the smoke screen surrounding this place. It was Catholic run, but had been attacked by the IRA with a large car bomb, why? A regular casual meeting place for republicans, or was it more? I believed the place to be important to the IRA as a centre for activities. The 300lb bomb that we had disposed of in front of the hotel a few weeks after the deaths of the five soldiers had left me with a strong suspicion that it was never meant to explode. For me this bomb was a trick to make us think that the hotel was under threat and thus quell any concerns we might harbour about the activities there, in short, I didn't believe any of it. This was the IRA playing a game of sleight of hand. But like it or not this was to be the location of the meeting between the colonel and his supposed old comrade.

Two of us were detailed to find an Observation Post from where we were able to keep Colonel Walker covered. I didn't think there was enough of us, we would need five or six guys with assault rifles if my fears where proven right. But we were stuck with what we had and until he actually arrived we didn't know which of the three hotel car parks was to be the venue. As we drove into the main car park in our thinly disguised Q car, the other Int soldier, Davy Steel, and I became aware of two cars, each with three male occupants mixed amongst the other vehicles, as if separate from each other and waiting for someone to leave the hotel. The occupants of these vehicles looked to me, hard and focused. My suspicions were immediately aroused and I could taste the adrenaline in my mouth.

Apart from the main car park which stood immediately in front of the hotel facade, the other two that we could see were terraced into woodland on the gentle slope of a hillside to its right. We had discussed our tactics before arriving. Two of us with our Browning pistols and nine rounds each had no chance of fighting off an ambush pressed

287

aggressively with assault rifles or worse. So instead of setting up a hide we decided to play our own game.

We assumed that any potential attackers, like us, would have to see which car park he decided to take before setting up an ambush. We planned to use a bluff to make it look like there were more of us than just the two and that we that we had much larger teeth than in fact we had. When Colonel Walker's car arrived on the road up to the car parks we toured the main car park in our Q car looking as sinister as possible, eyeballing all the men still sat in the two cars and speaking over an imaginary radio to other nonexistent undercover soldiers. Davy Steel said, "Did you see their faces, they looked uneasy?" "Forget their faces, just look at my fucking hand," I replied, holding a gently shaking appendage in front of my face, we both burst out laughing.

The CO had chosen the third car park that was furthest away from the hotel for their meeting as it was empty, so we parked out of sight in the second. Keeping a weather eye behind us in the direction of the main car park and the hotel, in case of any developments, we then started moving about in a pseudo tactical fashion in order to be seen by everyone other than Colonel Walker and his companion; the idea of this being to deter attack, in belief that we were part of a larger force. The two cars with the men in, plus another that we hadn't noticed before, sped off together on the exit road to our left. We then settled down to observing the CO and hoping he would hurry up so that we could move from our positions lying in the wet grass and observe their distant movements from our car.

I wasn't privy to the de brief, but I believe it wasn't much of a successful meeting. I'll never know whether my fears were right about a set up, unless that is someone in the IRA phones me up at this present time to tell me? 003401633------ I'll tell you the rest later!

A few months after that event, in Broderick's bar, which had been the site for the first supposed meeting with the Old Comrade; Special Branch officer Peter Flanagan was murdered by Sean O'Callaghan. Peter, who was to be my controller on my planned return as a civilian undercover agent with Alpha, was sat at the bar just about where I had sat that evening. Sean walked in through the door and emptied his revolver into him, killing him on the spot.

Lieutenant Colonel Anthony Walker eventually achieved the highest peacetime rank in the British Army. Full General, and became a knight of the realm. One of my sources told me that in early '74 an operation by an IRA hit team went to Knock-na-moe Castle Hotel to capture or kill a high ranking British officer. The operation went wrong when they detected what was described as an SAS counter ambush, and they had apparently aborted the operation.

Mike's Mullen & M Division Special Branch

The Special Branch team in Omagh in the early seventies consisted of four highly trained police officers and an Army Intelligence officer. There job being jointly to gather intelligence on the activities and movements of terrorists in the part of the province covered by police division ´M´, that being the south western part of county Tyrone. Where appropriate, Mike would pass on sections of this accrued data to us in order that the troops on the ground and any special forces in our area where able to be deployed in the most effective manner. This exchange of intelligence took place in both directions between the Army and the Police, with Mike Mullen mainly acting as the conduit.

I am therefore going to some of these events from their viewpoint which will hopefully add another, and different perspective. I shall endeavour to describe these activities in as accurate a way as I can. As always with these matters though, a great deal of human emotion can be involved. It would detract from the accurate picture of these tumultuous and often frightening events if I didn't occasionally touch on these very hard feelings.

On the night of Friday the 18th of May 1973 Mike

was in the Knock Na Mo Castle hotel, it was the night when the IRA murdered four soldiers by placing a booby trapped bomb under their car. He must have been one of the last people to see them alive. His car was parked in the car park where the bombing took place. The eighty pound bomb exploded under the car that five soldiers were about to leave in and two days later he was part of the special branch team who arrested Hugh Gerard Coney for the murder of the four soldiers who died on the night of the attack, the remaining victim didn't die until several days later. Coney was captured by a patrol of the Royal Hampshire Regiment, who had been briefed to watch out for him visiting his girlfriend's home. Mike remembers vividly them taking their prisoner back to Omagh police station and seeing his reaction as the colour drained from his face when they drove off route through the Knock Na Moo car park. Coney was, according to Mike, the most chillingly sinister man he ever met, a cold blooded killer who's callous disregard for human life put him in a class of his own, even though at that time and in that place they were in plentiful supply.

He was interrogated for the full seventy two hours without saying a single word and when Coney was delivered by the SB team to his inevitable, long term incarceration he turned to Mike and said, "I know you, your Ginge the Military intelligence officer," and continued, "when I get out I'm going to find and kill you". He then turned to each of the two

Special Branch officers who were also present and accurately named them, adding for each of the men that when he got out, he would kill them. Coney was subsequently shot and killed himself, whilst trying to escape from the Maze Prison. When, some months later, Mike heard the news of Coney's demise, from the Captain GSO3 Intelligence at 3 Brigade Head Quarters, he couldn't help but feel relieved.

In the early days of Captain Mike's work as the Military Intelligence Officer for the Royal Ulster Constabulary's "M' Division the team of four special branch offices with whom he was to work made it quite clear to him that they weren't prepared to share intelligence and contacts with anyone who wasn't prepared to share the same risks that they and their families had to take. This meant having to live outside the relative protection of the camp. Mike accepted this reality and during the next eighteen months, was forced to move home 3 times when the IRA caught up with him. Culminating in their murdering the wrong man in a botched up IRA operation which was supposed to end up with Mike on the mortuary slab, but more of that later. The SB team that Mike worked along with was headed by Inspector Peter Flanagan, a Catholic police officer whom I have written quite extensively about, earlier in this narrative. Peter had been a thorn in the side of the IRA since the previous (border) campaign.

The other members of the team where, Owen M, also a Catholic and two protestants, Denis A and Billy M. Mike who was also a Catholic, made up the final member of this elite team of three Catholics and two Protestants and constituted the team's link with the army including special forces.

As with my friend John Doc, a Catholic police officer who's brutal murder I detailed earlier in this history, anyone who was identified as a Catholic and who worked for the security forces was under particular threat of retribution, from the IRA. In Mike's case, the fact that he was a military intelligence officer added to his value as a target, so Ginge, as he was known to the IRA along with Peter Flanagan featured very high on the terrorists to do list. In the case of Peter, there was also a deeply personal reason why the IRA leadership wanted him dead.

At this point we need to regress 15 years to a night in1959, when a section of IRA volunteers came under attack from a mixed unit of Royal Ulster Constabulary and members of the infamous B Specials. During the ensuing gun fight David O'Connell, the commander of the IRA flying column was seriously injured when hit by fourteen bullets from the security forces Sten guns. The leader of the police during this successful ambush was a young Catholic police Sergeant called Peter Flanagan. Now, all these years later, Peter was head of Special

Branch for 'M' police division and David O'Connell was the Chief of Staff of the Provisional IRA. The animosity between these men wasn't just professional, it was deeply personal. O'Connell was just about to take things to a whole new level, by commissioning Peter's execution. The scene was now set for another brutal killing.

But before this could happen the IRA decided to have a crack at Mike. The Provisional leadership must have felt under a lot of pressure from this very successful Special Branch team who had extensive contacts within Tyrone's Catholic community and wanted this Omagh based unit totally destroyed. As previously mentioned Mike had to keep moving house in order to keep one step ahead of the butchers of the IRA. By late march 1974 he was living with his dog on the Mountfield Road in Omagh, close by to an ex infantry major who worked as a civilian in the towns Army Careers Office. Both these men had dogs and both of them were about the same build and stature. The IRAs reconnaissance for this kill operation was completed and the relevant information was taken across the border into the republic by the head of the CYM na Bahn, a political organisation which supported the IRA, by one of its leaders, a woman who lived in the village of Beragh. She was quite familiar with Mike as she worked has a servant in a house where Mike occasionally socialised. The job of killing Mike was passed onto Seamus Mallon and one other and the final reconnaissance for the operation was undertaken by members of the IRAs Carickmore Active Service Unit. On the day of the kill, Mallon and his sidekick followed the man who had been pointed out to them.

As expected the man took is dog in his car, what they didn't expect was that he stopped to feed some fishes. At which point the two volunteers opened fire killing both man and dog, with their new Kalashnikov AK47 assault rifle, this was the first time that this weapon was ever used in Ulster. The AK was courtesy of Colonel Muammar Gaddafi of Libya and had come as part of a large shipment of weapons.

They had killed the wrong man. It was a case of mistaken identity, the man they had killed was the retired officer, Don Farrell.

The note that had been secreted across the border in the woman's shoe was delivered to 22 Park Street in Monoghan: She delivered the note, from where it was later snatched during a Garda raid and handed to Dennis A, the Omagh SB sergeant. The note read, "The Military Intelligence Officer is ginger bald headed has a pointer dog and lives on Mountfield Rd" (the common colloquialism for Dalmatians like Mike's, in that part of Ireland was 'Pointy Dog'). Poor Don Farrell was butchered by mistake.

Then on the 23 August of that year Peter Flanagan's turn arrived. David O'Connel selected a young man who had recently been working as part of the Carickmore Active Service Unit, to kill Peter. Sean O'Callaghan had been personally selected and briefed. Two helpers were assigned to him, a woman driver for the car they where to steal, and an extra gun man, both were from Belfast. O'Callaghan had been given a brand new 3.57mm magnum pistol, which had never been used before. Somehow Sean had managed to stay off the intelligence radar. I do remember him being discussed but only as a youth who was known to be on the run after blowing up his parent's home, while practising his bomb making skills. No one ever suggested that he was in Ulster, never mind that he was skulking around in our division, but this up and coming star had been selected to play the role of Peter's executioner.

The IRAs plan was that the Belfast man would glance through the doorway to make certain that Peter was there, he would then give Sean an all clear nod and stay outside guarding the getaway route. Sean would then enter and kill Peter.
Broderick's Bar was and is situated only a few meters away and to the left of the court house in Omagh where it partially closes off the end of the town's main shopping street. In those days there was no free access for motor vehicles to the high

street but it was possible by driving along nearby streets to reach the unmanned barriers that barred access from the side streets. After the shooting, they would swiftly retreat on foot to one of these barriers where the girl was sat in the car with its engine running.

What the IRA intelligence hadn't told them was that although Inspector Flannigan would often appear to be alone during his nightly vigil at the bar; in fact Mike was often sat behind a wind break from where he was able to cover both doors with his own personal weapon. He would not allow them to reach Peter.

 Unfortunately on the night things didn't work out so simple.

Mike had to visit Lisanely Camp that afternoon, to brief the Commanding Officer there about the current intelligence situation. This meeting was dragging on longer than initially planned and Mike needed to cut and run if he was to keep his usual appointment with Peter Flannigan, but by the time he got away, he was half an hour late and Peter was already dead.

As O'Callaghan walked into the pub holding the pistol in front of him, Peter who was sat at the bar jumped to his feet, and holding his hands away from himself in a kind of defensive gesture shouted "no no". Peter then tried to turn and run towards the toilets but O'Callaghan opened fire, pumping round after round into his prone body, until his weapon was empty. Bizarrely, O'Callaghan just stood there and reloaded the weapon with new rounds of ammunition that he was carrying in his pocket and stooping over the dying Peter Flannigan, he reached down and fired another two rounds into the back of Peters head, then walked out. Unfortunately, Peter had gone to his meeting with Mike leaving his personal defence weapon in his office and Mike had been delayed. Therefore Peter, had no means of defending himself. After the killing, O'Callaghan sped back off to his hideaway at Carickmore's priest's house and remained undetected until he walked into a police station on the UK mainland years later and confessed to this killing along with others.

End Game

My military service was moving towards its conclusion. During the weeks before my leaving the army I had again discussed at length with Mike Mullen regarding my returning to Ireland as a civilian undercover operative, for which purpose I had recruited Alpha. The arrangements that I had made in Ireland were: Alpha and I would return from the mainland after a few months had elapsed and collect intelligence in both the Republic and in the north. Both sides of the border would be our domain and we would be tasked by Omagh Special Branch.

The work in Ireland continued until my very last day. In late April, having found no one to take me to Belfast for my ferry, I caught the public bus service from Omagh. I was finished with the army and had handed everything of issue back to them. Last of all, my personal weapon was handed in at the arms store. My plan was to take the ferry from Belfast to Liverpool and then catch a train from Liverpool to London where it was necessary to meet some people. Then I would continue my journey to Nottingham where I would meet up with Sinead. In the event, I stayed in London for six weeks before continuing my journey north to my loved one in Nottingham.

While in the capital I found a job in a pub called the Green Man & French Horn on Saint Martin's Lane in the West End. My life felt empty and pointless, all those people living their normal lives and passing me by without a glance. Their comfortable existence's chaffed against my battered soul. The fire was still raging inside me and I deeply resented their perfect lives. How was I to wake them up to what was happening in the world? The pain and horror of it; they didn't seem capable of its comprehension. I was full of anger and resentment and many bitter memories and for some strange reason blamed their carefree existence for the world's sickness.

  This was no place for me! Even though I had only ever spent one weekend in Nottingham, it was the place where I needed to go. Sinead was there; I missed her closeness and needed her strength to help fight my demons.

In June of 1974 I headed north.

By this time I had run out of money and although Nottingham was a less impersonal city when compared with London, it was still hard on paupers, so I set to finding myself a job, any job. With very little effort I found work as a night security guard for a company called Armaguard based in West Bridgford, just across the Trent Bridge from Nottingham. The pay was poor and the hours were lousy, but it was enough to give me a subsistence lifestyle for a while. I was able to find accommodation in a shared house on London Road in the city, near to the Nottingham Forest football ground.

The house had once been a shop but was now run down to the point of dilapidation and was split into four bed sitting rooms with a communal lounge area. Sinead and I met when it was possible, but with both of us working shifts it wasn't easy.

Through TV and newspapers and the occasional phone call to friends, I kept in touch the best that I could with what was happening in Fermanagh and Tyrone. But I was now living in a different world where none of the values that I had come to hold dear seemed to matter a damn. People seemed to be living their insular lives with little regard for how it affected others and responsibility seemed to extend only to the edge of their tight families and close friends. There was a deep festering resentment growing within me for their endemic selfishness that seemed to be the order of the day.
By this time I was being constantly haunted by

intrusive memories of warfare. They filled my every moment of repose, and I was finding even normal socialising difficult. There was a deep anger smouldering inside my chest. How could this be the end? There was so much left to do to defeat the IRA. This was not a conclusion, there was still so much more to be done. My whole being was focused on the destruction of my enemies; it seemed just a matter of time.

Sinead stuck by me and stayed out of trouble, having seemingly put her political and military aspirations to one side for the moment. I was so full of love and admiration for this tough, little lady and so confused about my own feelings, that I felt that I must take positive action to continue with my destiny and follow my fate to the endgame.

It was a Saturday evening in late June when we met on Trent Bridge. I held her in my arms and kissed the side of her face and held her tight to me. Powerful emotions were coursing through my entire body. I needed to tell her a lie but didn't want her to see it in my eyes. When we parted that night she thought that I had met someone else. I watched her for the last time as she walked across the bridge towards where she had parked her car in Bridgford. I watched her and her wet reflection on the pavement as she walked away without as much as a backwards glance. There was no other woman, and it would be thirty six years before we would meet again.

After I came away from Ireland the regiment soldiered on for another three months, during which time the security situation stayed acute.

The weeks after I left Ireland on the 20th of May were very hectic for those RTR soldiers who were left behind. The number of serious attacks in their area didn't ease off at all. But on the 16th of June, the day that I became a civilian again, a little light relief was felt when the ATO was called out to perform a controlled explosion on a suitcase that had been left on the Omagh to Cookstown road, near Omagh. Calls from members of the public brought the suitcase to the attention of the police, who contacted the army and a massive cordon operation sprang into effect. Once it was certain that members of the local population were shielded from the blast effect of this substantial sized potential bomb, the ATO went to work on it.

There was now no danger to people or property so the ATO decided that the safest way to deal with a device like this one was to use a controlled explosion to disrupt any timing or 'anti lift' mechanism that it might contain. A few ounces of PE4 were placed against it and when everyone was clear, it was detonated with spectacular effect.

It transpired that the suitcase had been left on the road by accident, when a priest had stopped his car to sort out his luggage. Something had distracted the good father's attention and he ended up driving away without replacing the suitcase into his car. What was thought to be a bomb, turned out to be vestments and other priestly paraphernalia, all of which was unfortunately destroyed by the blast. After his eventful Sunday the ATO didn't have to wait long before he had more work to do. It was just twenty four hours later when Lisnaskea, in county Fermanagh, was attacked.

Shortly after 11.30 at night a 1 RTR foot patrol on Main Street in the town were told about a car bomb which was outside Leekies Bar. The patrol had a frantic 30 minutes clearing the area in time. It exploded with devastating effect at just gone midnight.

The following day, the 18th of June, saw an incident in which a UDR patrol stopped a car which was crossing the border from the Republic and was on its way to Newtownbutler. When stopped by the patrol, the driver of the vehicle switched on one of his indicators as a signal to the remainder of his active service unit, who were following at a distance behind him. When the driver was instructed to switch his indicators off, he refused. Within a few seconds another car coming from the same direction screeched to a halt some distance short of the VCP and the men inside took off on foot across the fields, heading back towards the Republic.

The members of the patrol, who were from 4 UDR, instigated a search of the car that the men had run from. The driver of the car that the patrol had stopped first was held prisoner. Explosives were found in both vehicles.

During that same week a car bomb exploded without warning at Rosslea in county Fermanagh, seriously damaging both the local school and the police station and injuring three people.
What had started off as an amusing week with the suitcase on the previous Sunday was now turning into one of the worst weeks that the regiment had had for incidents, when on the following Friday a post office van was hijacked on the Tyrone Monaghan border by armed men. They placed two milk churns in the back of the van and told the driver to take it to Robinson's hardware shop in Clogher. A 1 hour warning was received which enabled security forces to evacuate the area before the 100lb bomb detonated at 11.30 causing severe damage to several shops and houses in the town and breaking windows over a large area. Once again The 1st Royal Tank Regiment where at the centre of the response to all these events.

On the 25th of June the terrorists returned to Omagh. Once again the Crown buildings in the town were targeted by a 250lb proxy car bomb. Brian Ward, the driver of the van, was doing repair work on the Crown Buildings after a previous attack. Brian, a Carrickmore man, had had his van hijacked before; the van was subsequently used to deliver a bomb to Market Street, in Omagh. That bomb in the previous January had caused a great deal of destruction in the town. This time, after the bomb was loaded into it, he was instructed to drive his vehicle through the town's security cordon and park up behind the Crown Buildings. After following his instructions he informed security forces and helped to warn members of the public. The bomb exploded an hour later, causing much damage to the Crown Buildings and destroying a nearby poultry building and in doing so covered half of Omagh centre with feathers and fresh chicken portions.

The troubles went on and on without me, day after day, atrocity after atrocity, the towns and villages of the two counties were being destroyed. Those IRA attacks were meant to break the region's economy and strike fear into the hearts of its people.

Not to be left out, Castlederg was next on the terrorists list when on the 6th of July a taxi was hijacked by armed men on the outskirts of the village. After the bomb had been placed in the taxi, the driver was told to drive it to the Lyons garage on Strabane Road in Castlederg. The area was quickly cordoned off by security forces and the ATO sent for. Part of the bomb detonated and was set on fire by a controlled explosion. Fortunately, only a small amount of damage was done by that device.

When I heard about the escalation of events in Ireland, I was chomping at the bit to get back there, but I had to bide my time and wait. I took a keen interest in the regiment's continuing activities, which included quelling a riot in Carrickmore after a republican pub had been blown up.

 But the event that caught my interest the most, and really got my juices going, was when a Command Troop 1RTR observation post which was watching an illegal border crossing point were just recovering from a cold autumn night in their position when two cars travelling from the Republic pulled up on the Northern Ireland side of the border and four men climbed out of their cars. Three of the men were armed and the whole group started moving milk churns between the vehicles. The command troop soldiers couldn't believe their luck, they had caught an active service unit red handed. A warning was shouted for the men to drop their weapons and raise their hands. One of the quartet did just that but the others took to their heels in the direction of the nearby border. The soldiers opened fire on the fleeing terrorists, hitting one of them who fell to the ground. Because of the position of the two cars it was difficult to get a good aim at the remaining two fleeing men without hitting the one who had surrendered. So the soldiers satisfied themselves with the capture of the two that they had.

It turned out that the man who had surrendered immediately was an innocent member of the public who, along with his car, had been hijacked and the injured man, who was still lying in the road with two gunshot wounds, was a member of the IRA unit. The bombs were destined for the long suffering Castlederg. It is not known whether the two who escaped received any injuries.

  The start of the incident was at about 09.50 in the morning and the bomb that they had been handling exploded about an hour later, while the two captives were being treated and questioned. The other bomb was found to consist of approximately 400 lbs of explosive.

On Friday August 30th, Kinawley came under attack when a 300 lb car bomb exploded in front of the local police station, destroying it and damaging many homes and businesses in the vicinity. A young farmer was made to deliver this bomb while his wife and children where held hostage by the terrorists. The small towns and villages of Fermanagh and Tyrone were starting to creek under the pressure of this sustained bombing campaign. Some of these villages housed less than a couple of hundred families but where hit over and over again. On it went into October until, on the 10th of the month, soldiers who were on duty over the election period and carrying out a routine patrol along the country lane were travelling eastwards away from Kinawley when the explosion occurred.

The force of the explosion, caused by an estimated 300lb mine placed in a culvert under the road, blew the Land Rover on its side and caused a crater three feet deep.

Cpl Tom Gaskell was driving the vehicle with Cpl Ray Bradley in the passenger seat. Troopers John Riding and Derek Leek were in the rear of the Land Rover.

None of the soldiers can recall hearing the explosion which hurled their vehicle through the air and on to its side. Cpl's Bradley and Gaskell remembered looking at each other as they flew through the air before they found themselves trapped underneath the vehicle. The force of the blast had blown in the passenger door which trapped Cpl Bradley's left leg pinning him under the Land Rover. His watch was blown off his wrist. Cpl Bradley yelled at Gaskell to get out. "I can't," replied Gaskell. "Undo your bloody seatbelt, it's easier," replied Bradley. Cpl Gaskell extricated himself from the Land Rover and then, using his SLR to raise the door, pulled Cpl Bradley clear of the wreckage. Trooper John Riding assisted Gaskell in ripping off Bradley's burning trousers and dragged him along the road to safety. Bradley later complained of gravel rash on his backside.

They could afford to laugh because in spite of their

narrow brush with death they had escaped with few injuries.

Cpl Gaskell received blast damage to his chest, a bruised chin and required several stitches to a head wound. Cpl Bradley had severe lacerations to his right leg that required stitching, and gravel rash. Trooper Riding bruised his knee and had two stitches in his right cheek and trooper Leek required stitches in his cut forearm and knee. This was Leek's second escape from serious injury: in 1972 in Lergan, a sniper's bullet pierced the butt of his SLR wounding the man next to him.

Cpl Bradley's watch was recovered from the crater and was found to have stopped at 10.55. The exact time of the explosion that nearly killed him and his comrades. Throughout their ordeal the four soldiers' behaviour had been commendable and the fact that they were able to laugh it off is a tribute to their courage and high morale.

Within moments of the soldiers getting clear, the petrol tank ignited and with a terrific roar the vehicle blew up. A number of civilians appeared on the scene and Cpl Gaskell kept them clear as the ammunition aboard started to explode. Gaskell with great calmness then proceeded to organise first aid, bandaging his comrades with shell dressings, and later marshalled the RAF Puma helicopter that evacuated them.

On arrival at Erne Hospital, Enniskillen, the four soldiers were taken to the casualty department. They were seated, awaiting their turn for treatment when a nurse approached them and said that she had some bad news. She informed them in a quiet, caring voice that one of them had died during the incident! The four battered warriors covered in blood and dust looked at each other and then burst out laughing, much to the confused women's discomfort. She then went scuttling off to find her informant and hopefully get her message straightened out.

September broke with a flurry when on the 1st of the month a family from the Republic were captured and held hostage by terrorists. The incident started when Joseph Boyle from the county of Donegal in the Republic was driving his young family in their car near Clady in county Londonderry. The car was stopped by armed men who then took both the family and the car back across the border to a farm in Donegal where a bomb was loaded into the vehicle. Joseph was told that his wife and two children, a girl of seven and a boy of five, would be held hostage until he delivered the car bomb to the newly repaired police HQ at Newtownstewart in county Tyrone just north east of Omagh. With his family in the hands of these terrorists, Joseph had no option but to follow their instructions and drive the car bomb to its target across the border.

On arrival at Newtownstewart Police Barracks he abandoned the vehicle and started shouting warnings to people nearby. There were many people running to clear the area, all, that is but one!

An Ulster Defence Regiment soldier who was on duty just climbed into the vehicle and drove it the short distance to a field, where twenty minutes later the car exploded harmlessly. The Garda later found the man's family safe and well.

When the UDR soldier was later asked why he had taken the chance to move the bomb away from the buildings he said that so much work had been done there after the last attack and he didn't want to have to paint the bastard again!

This incident was unusual on two counts. Firstly, it was not normal for the IRA to involve citizens of the Republic in their attacks and secondly in the way the Garda showed more than their usual mild interest in these events. On this occasion they acted in, what seemed from a far, a professional way?

On the tour's completion in mid November, members of the regiment and attached personnel were awarded more than twenty gallantry awards and medals for their part in the campaign while I looked on from afar awaiting my return to the fight.

By the end of the tour, approximately sixty bombs consisting of more than 20,000lb of explosives had been planted in our two police divisions and dealt with by us. A large percentage of these devices had been aimed at members of the regiment and their families. More than fifty, Soviet built RPG 7 Anti Tank rockets and dozens of mortar shells, had been fired at them during attacks and thousands of rounds of ammunition, using everything from machine guns, rifles and handguns, but the most dangerous weapon that the IRA deployed against us was stealth.

The three Squadrons of 1RTR, consisting of about three hundred and fifty men in total completed this long tour, mostly performing tasks that were outside their normal operational role. It was a great tribute to the regiment that they were able to change from that of manoeuvring tanks to a full infantry and reconnaissance role.

They acted most courageously under the most trying and stressful conditions thinkable. Keeping up the highest traditions of the British Army throughout the eighteen months of that tour, both the soldiers and their families came under constant attack from the bombs and bullets of the IRA.

My time back in England was becoming a dismal affair. At first, and for awhile, I felt relieved to be away from it all, but it wasn't too long before a feeling of guilt overtook me, and that old gut feeling that I should be back in Ireland. In my mind I was letting the side down by not being there and doing my job. There was a deep resentment of the frivolity of other peoples' cosy civilian lives smouldering inside me. Didn't they know what was going on over there, and if they did, did they care? I was bitter and angry as well as being profoundly saddened by the great feeling of loss that was overtaking me.

Away from the immediate dangers of life under threat, I was able to take a proper look at myself, and what I saw wasn't impressive. I was hyper defensive and constantly looking over my shoulder and preparing for the next attack. My first reaction to being in any public place was to work out an exit strategy and I would check out all the potential weapons that were available to me. Anything that I could use in my defence was noted and assessed. All routes of escape were looked at and checked for viability. This tedious process was gone through with every new location that I found myself in and on top of all this my feelings of guilt at having survived became more and more obtrusive.

I no longer had Sinead in my life so I just kept working towards my return to the fight.
The money I was earning had improved and I quite enjoyed my new line of work. I had picked up a job in a small engineering company. They were involved in manufacturing batches of machine components. It

was all subcontracted work, brought in from larger engineering companies, in and around the city. I was to operate a centre lathe on the night shift. The last time that I had operated any kind of a lathe was fourteen years previously when I was only fifteen years old and then I had only done it very briefly as an apprentice in Oldham. I had talked them into giving me a job on the strength of this vast experience which I had slightly, only slightly exaggerated.

Arriving for my first shift, I approached the great sullen looking, nineteenth century factory building which cut across a small stream that flowed between two other dark industrial structures. The murky waters of the stream flowed in the direction of the canal which flanked London Road, near to Trent Bridge. The entrance to the building was guarded by two great wooden doors which were painted green and were rotting away at their bottoms. The building was about four stories high but only the ground floor was used by the engineering company, the rest of the building being at various stages of dilapidation.
The workshop that revealed itself when I entered, was large enough for up to fifty people to work in with lathes and milling machines, drill stands and fitters work benches. There were other machines there as well that I didn't recognise. They looked fully automated and were probably worth hundreds

of thousands of pounds.

My machine was to be an old centre lathe which was situated next to another lathe that the only other night shift worker operated. It felt rather strange that only the two of us were to work the shift. My co-worker introduced himself as Peter. He showed me the work that I was expected to do and then conscientiously bent back over his machine to continue his work load. I hadn't got a clue.

It was 6 pm when we started work and by the time 4 am rolled around my body clock was protesting about my having not retired to bed several hours before. It reminded me of nights on long ops where I was trying my best to maintain some kind of interest in the job at hand, whilst not giving in to my natural inclination. Sleep!

I didn't achieve very much work wise, but no one seemed to worry about that, the main thing was that I was there making up the vital number for a night shift, which was the grand total of two.

It was still dark when I walked home to my bedsit after completing my first twelve hour night shift and within minutes of climbing into my bed, I was fast asleep.

The noise of the traffic outside started to creep into my consciousness and I lay for a long time wondering what time it was. When eventually I reached for my watch, I couldn't believe my weary eyes. It was nine fifteen in the morning and the traffic on the busy road outside was thundering by at the peak of the rush hour. I had four of these shifts to complete every week and if I was not able to get a proper, decent sleep, I would struggle to achieve them. Maybe I could bring forward our Irish project, or should I go to Oldham for a few months until we were ready to go. I found the night shifts very difficult, but at least when the weekend eventually came around, I had a little money to get by on.

Although I struggled with the night shift hours, I had no intention of staying there for more than a few months, so it didn't matter to me much. I had only been working in the job for a few weeks when I decided to take an impromptu sicky in order to go to the pub. Nothing much was expected of me on these shifts but I was finding the constant nights hard. The daytime when I was supposed to sleep was full of traffic noise thanks to the location of my grotty little bed sit, and if truth was known I was missing Sinead like hell. Anyway, it all got too much and I just thought, to hell with it and instead of going to work one night, I took a different turn and went to the pub.
I felt guilty about my workmate who wasn't supposed to be working on his jack; it being down to some kind of a health and safety rule, I suppose. It felt good though at eleven o'clock when I was

walking home, knowing that I was going to bed instead of working all night. I remember thinking that I needed to get another job to get away from those shifts.

The three Special Branch officers, who were waiting for me in the shared sitting room, had been let in by one of the other occupants of the house. They were here to investigate an incident that had taken place at the engineering factory earlier that evening. It appeared that when I failed to arrive for work, my workmate had decided to work his normal shift and was surprised when he looked up from his machine to discover that he was in the company of four large Irish men.

They had broken in through the locked Main Entrance expecting to find me there. When this was told to me, my first thought was for Sinead, and was she OK. I knew instantly that it wasn't her who had put the finger on me. For starters she didn't know where I was working, as we had parted before I got the new job, but she did know where I lived. These men on the other hand, had been trying to break into the works offices in order to find out my address so they must have been keen to find me.

My terrified workmate was told that if he called the police he would be shot. My mind had difficulty comprehending how the hell they had found me so far from the places that I would be normally expected to be. It crossed my mind that they had gone to a lot of trouble to have located me so quickly, especially as I barely existed in the murky subculture of Nottingham's back streets. Once again I became deeply concerned for Sinead in case those people that had found me would present a greater problem for her. The Special Branch officers with Detective Constable Nigel Stacy taking the lead attempted to question me at great length, but I refused to give them anything but the name and phone number of Mike Mullen in Ireland, and the name of SB Inspector Peter Flanagan in Omagh. This frustrated them greatly and one of them started getting tough with me. His manner became aggressive and his body language threatening. At this point I told them to either charge me with something or "fuck off." Realising that there was nothing for them to charge me with and failing to get any more cooperation from me, they decided upon the latter option. When they had gone I thought hard about my situation, I needed to get out of there that night. So I grabbed the few bits that I had and tossed them into my car, and then drove away and slept in the car that night in a pub car park.

In the afternoon of the following day I ventured back to my bed sit to make sure I had got all of my valuable possessions, only to discover that DC Stacy was there waiting for me. His attitude was markedly different than on the previous evening. He had obviously made enquiries of the two contacts that I had given him. Stacy was concerned that my tormenters would catch up with me. I assured him that I intended to take a powder and disappear well below the radar. He indicated that he wanted to have a talk with me somewhere private and insisted that I take his work phone number. I accepted it but told him that I had plans and that I wouldn't be side tracked.

We parted on good terms and I disappeared into the primeval soup of Nottingham's back streets. Each night I parked my car, which was crammed with all my worldly goods, in one or other of the pub car parks and tried to sleep. My legs became stiff and I was cold, anything more than an occasional nap was impossible and the bit of money that I had soon started to run out. I washed in public toilets or pubs and tried to keep my clothes clean by way of occasional visits to a laundrette but both my physical and mental condition had started to take a nose dive.

At the age of twenty nine years and after serving my country, I was living like a tramp. I knew no one and had to keep on the move, but there was one powerful motivation that kept me going. Like some kind of automaton my prime directive was to damage the IRA. I needed to keep my head down for now, so I continued my vagrant lifestyle for several more weeks until eventually I picked up a new job working for an industrial sewing machine manufacturers. The job gave me the incentive and finance to also find accommodation in the scruffy Hyson Green area of Nottingham. It wasn't up to much, but was marginally better than the back seat of my Ford Anglia.

Weeks later when I re-contacted Nigel Stacy, he suggested that he take me for a drink as he had a little project to discuss and I agreed.

The talk that we had proved to be the start of over six years of undercover work for Special Branch in Nottingham. I told Nigel that I was committed to a project in Ireland and that it must have priority and he agreed. The work that I was involved in Special Branch meant that I was positively vetted and was required to sign copies of the official secrets act with great regularity. Accordingly, I can not divulge the nature of that work.

Or can I?

In the event Ireland never came off. I became aware through TV news that Inspector Peter Flanagan of Omagh Special Branch who was to be my contact, had been shot dead in Broderick's Bar on 23 August by Sean O'Callaghan, who was at that time a member of the Provisional IRA. Mike Mullen who was my remaining contact after the Regiment had left had been promoted to major and moved on to a TA battalion in Northampton.

The whole Ireland venture was to be risky enough without the added complication of a new controller who I didn't know and therefore I thought hard about whether or not to continue. It was a decision that only I could make and I didn't feel that I could trust anyone that I didn't know with both of our lives. I told Alpha that the job was on hold for the time being and he went off to Africa as a mercenary.

At that stage it was very hard for me to know what to do, but I recognised that I needed to change direction. All those lives ended so violently, wasted as if they had no worthwhile value at all. How were we able to do this to each other? No simple answer. Friend's lost forever, comrades never to be seen again. Some were lost for the sake of a cause and others destroyed in order for someone to make a point. Staff Sergeant Ron Becket, a big, strong man with a jolly smile and father to a young family. And yes, a very close friend. He was the second bomb disposal officer that I worked alongside and thankfully the only one to be killed. There was Brian Criddle and his faithful partner, Jason. Brian was awarded the British Empire Medal just days before he was killed by the IRA in a carefully laid trap. He was also a father and husband. This explosive tracker dog team had worked unrelentingly from virtually the start of the IRA campaign. After almost three years detecting explosives it was only a matter of time before he was caught out. And has he lain bleeding and mortally injured on the ground, he could hear the IRA mob laughing and calling triumphantly from their safe haven in the republic, not 300 yards away.

There were many others. My great friend John Docherty, butchered in his car while visiting his mother in the republic by men who were not fit to lick his boots. I remember John telling me that there was no courage without fear, John would know, he was a man of enormous courage. Like Detective Inspector Peter Flanagan, the Special Branch officer who I was to report my spying activities too. Shot dead in a public house in Omagh. The list seems endless. Derek Reed, the army helicopter pilot who was killed along with four of his mates on the very day I arrived in Ireland. Their booby trapped car presented to me a shocking introduction to the Irish way of doing things. The list goes on, all of them men and women that I either knew or dealt with in some way. There was Intelligence Officer Captain McCabe and Private Eve Martin, both of the Ulster Defence Regiment. I didn't know them well in life but their deaths left a vivid impression on me. Eve was at that time the only female soldier to be killed during the campaign. But that distinction would be soon lost. I remember her from previous visits to the Deanery where she sometimes worked in the operations room. She was a beautiful woman, always friendly and helpful, so unlike the ragged corpse with horrific head injuries lying on the stairs at the Deanery. I see it in my mind's eye now: all the victims of executions and the people whose lives were terminated by bombs. How could we do this? No simple answer. The ragged, lifeless puppets of men destroyed in body and those left with Mutilated Minds. This was the greatest achievement of the IRA campaign, which I for one had to carry away with me.

List of Special Branch Officers that I worked with from 1974 onwards:
DC Nigel Stacy 1974
DC Dave Cowlishaw late 1975 on
Inspector Bruce Foster 1978 on
Chief Inspector Jeff Greenaway
And a mysterious man called Bernard from Carshalten, who whenever I met him dropped the 'in' term 'Desk' into the conversation. I decided that he was MI5.
There were several other Officers whose names I can't now remember. Most of these Officers worked out of Nottinghamshire Police HQ at Burnt Stump Park.

The now Major Mike Mullen caused a bit of a flurry a couple of years later by finding me through SB contacts. He wanted to know how I was getting on with things; out of respect I told him that everything was OK. I assumed that he had used SB contacts to locate me. His enquiry was passed on to me and he and I spoke on the telephone, but I got the impression from SB that his interest had caused some fidgeting at Burnt Stump. Perhaps they thought I would want to go off to war again?

For me my service had ended, but for many others it hadn't even started. There were to be people not even born yet, who would die in these troubles. Day in and day out we had followed this trail of death and destruction across that beautiful, fresh clean land. The maiming and killing of friends and acquaintances became routine, and that of strangers, less important. On the surface it felt like there was no effect, but there was a price to be paid. We just didn't understand the currency yet.

How many times did we come close to being killed without even knowing it? How many dud bombs did we pass over on our travels? How many ambushes did we bypass on a whim? The gods of war were kind to most of us, others died.

During those sad years some of the most disgusting specimens of humanity disguised their activities under the cloak of republicanism, they worked with and alongside intellectuals and sharp business men, who did not find it hard to separate slaughter from the acquisition of wealth.

People like Slab Murphy who was one of the latter, made millions out of the division of Ireland through smuggling. This once Provisional Chief Of Staff had a vested interest in keeping those divisions in place. It's difficult for me to understand why none of the movement's intellectuals ever questioned this clash of interests, which was repeated again and again throughout the activities of the IRA. Perhaps they were too cowardly to face up to the monsters that they had created, or felt that they had to hide from the realities of it.

I want the shaky peace that now prevails in Ulster to grow and prosper. I want all of the scars to disappear. The Omagh bombing that took place on Saturday the fifteenth of August 1998 came as an enormous shock to the whole of the Northern Ireland community. The loss of those 29 precious lives meant that it was time to stop and think. This act of obscene violence had a powerful effect on how everyone viewed the sectarianism that had fathered it. All the bitterness of those past years started to melt and even the most hardened political bigots started to look towards a different horizon.

The towns and villages that I knew as communities at war, have now got a different dynamic that's driving their rejuvenation, it must be allowed to complete its work. Other scars will take longer to heal, especially those families with great rents in them from the loss of a member and the individuals who have had their hearts ripped out. I for one am still haunted by the ghosts of our comrades who gave their lives so courageously, as well as the many innocents whose futures were stolen by this conflict. It will take generations of both communities sending their kids to be educated in the same multi-religion schools, to repair that. But will it ever happen? Does history have to go on repeating itself? I was ever an optimist.

THE END

John Doherty RUC

In memory of all the casualties including

Truth

Peter Flanagon SB

Huge land mine blast (men standing at road level)

Ron Becket ATO

Brien Criddle & Jason

John Doherty helping when Ron was killed

Eve Martin

Captain Cormack McCabe

Epilogue

This may be the end of my personal story, but it is not the end of my opinions and certainly not the end of all the historical information. I owe a debt to some people and others deserve my condemnation. People who were once my sworn enemies and others, whom I classed as friends, can be seen in the light of their subsequent actions, both for good and evil. Notable amongst these is Sean O'Callaghan who I knew to be on the run and thought to be an IRA volunteer in our area. Sean became quite a success in the IRA and was involved in a great deal of activity in the south Tyrone area. He was implicated in two killings there, one of which was the murder of my soon to be controller, Special Branch Inspector Peter Flanagan and the other the killing of the beautiful Eve Martin. A recently acquired description of Peters execution which details Sean first of all emptying his gun into Peter and then standing over him whilst reloading, before firing a further two shots into the back of Peter Flanagan's head. In my view leaves Sean with a great residue of explanation which needs satisfying before I am prepared to fully except Sean's current anti terrorist philosophy.

 Never the less It would appear that at the point where he was making quite a name for himself, Sean developed a conscience, he became sickened and disgusted by both his own activities and those of his fellow volunteers in the IRA. After an extended period of self appraisal, Sean says that he decided that he was no longer able, in conscience, to continue his support for the cause that he had once felt so proud to represent. Instead of just walking away from it like a lesser man would do, he decided to pay for his own sins by doing his utmost to destroy the Provisional IRA. Sean volunteered to infiltrate the upper ranks of that organisation for Irish Special Branch and later for MI5. He later walked into a police station in the UK and gave himself up for the murders of both Inspector Flanagan and Eva Martin who was killed during the attack on our patrol base at The Deanery in Clougher. Sean was sentenced to over 500 years in prison for his offences, but was released 8 years later after receiving a Royal Pardon.

By the very nature of Irish Republicanism, any one speaking out loudly against them is in great danger of reprisals, but I for one am glad to stand shoulder to shoulder with this former enemy. Apart from the background and introduction of this work, most of the events and incidents detailed in this story

331

happened in one small area of Northern Ireland and constitute only a fraction of the complete picture. Soldiers and police officers in all parts of Ulster had to deal with similar situations. I accept that some of the more sinister aspects of the secret war against the IRA may be hard for liberal society to condone; I make no apology for any of my actions during this time, or for the actions of the brave men and women that I had the honour to work with. In these situations we do whatever it takes to win. The campaign along the border with the Irish Republic was often under reported at the time, but in my mind it was the crux of the whole situation. I don't believe that the troubles would have lasted half as long as they did, were it not for the Republic's insistence in trying to rewrite the Anglo Irish Treaty, to which they where signatories. Many of the small towns and villages that feature in my narrative had populations of only a few hundred people, and were themselves only thinly spread over a large rural area. Yet vast amounts of explosives were deployed against the inhabitants, over and over again. Places like Castlederg were hit repeatedly, yet still seemed to function. For me, this says volumes about the people who lived, and still live there.

The People

Lt Colonel Walker became General Sir Antony Walker KCB.

Major Mike Mullen MBE (this name has been changed to protect Mike's identity) spent a total of 37 years in the army, fulfilling many different roles with great distinction and when he heard about this book in early 2014 he contacted me.

Captain Holtom has only recently finished with the army. When his thirty odd years service were completed in 2006. Brigadier Chris Holtom retired as The Director of Army Intelligence. He now acts as a private contractor on both military and civil matters.

Davy Steele became a famous Scottish Folk Singer, born in 1948, died of cancer in 2001 and sadly missed by many.

Paddy Carrol was last heard of running a busy pub in Liverpool

Ron Woods now lives in retirement in the south of England and has learned not to swear so much!

David McEvoy lives somewhere in Spain.

Historical Notes Ireland

The shoot to kill policy

Undercover soldiering in Northern Ireland was a dangerous and desperate business. If this conflict had been classed as a war, according to the rules of warfare laid down in the Geneva Conventions, soldiers who operate out of uniform are classed the same as terrorists and it is legal for them to be summarily executed. As indeed where the six German soldiers who were captured on a mission in the United States early in the Second World War. In fact, under these circumstances the undercover soldier gives up many of his rights under the Geneva Convention. The convention states that combatants must wear a recognisable uniform with badges of rank and weapons must be carried openly. The IRA's status under these conventions is not that of a combatants but the indiscriminate nature of many of their killings rather points to terrorism than anything else. The IRA pitilessly tortured and slaughtered every single security forces member that fell into their grasp, but still employed some warped logic which both excused these murders and denied the security forces the right of self defence.

The IRA and its friends, in Ireland and in the UK, constantly accused the security forces of operating a shoot to kill policy. According to their beliefs and often stated propaganda, the army and police, but particularly the army operated under secret instructions to ruthlessly kill any IRA Volunteers that they came across. I don't think that they actually believed any of this.

Some soldiers through selection and training are more efficient and ruthless in the execution of their duties than others. But faced with an armed enemy most soldiers try to see them as a target, not as a man to be slaughtered. Once you bring your target's humanity into the equation, your natural instinct to protect, rather than slay, comes into play. It is true that specially selected and trained troops such as the S.A.S and others will often make a better job destroying their target, in order not to give it an opportunity to, for instance set off a bomb, or raise an alert. This kind of necessary ruthlessness comes at a high price to both recipient and donor. There are normally no feelings of deep enmity towards our enemies. We felt disgusted and horrified at some of the things that they did, but no more than that. I can remember feeling this at the many funerals of friends and comrades that I had the misfortune to have to attend.

That said, some particular terrorists who always

seemed to be under the protection of the Irish State, managed to develop a particular ruthless intent in me. A particular hatred felt personally and individually against those who always seemed to get away with it. Thanks to the Garda's seeming inability to respond to any attacks that did not take place on their own territory, many members of the IRA lived freely and openly in the Republic, and where often able to bathe in the glow of their infamy. Those that the Irish State did put away usually did easy time as so called political prisoners, no matter what the nature of the crimes that they committed.

There were numerous instances in my experience, where the security forces caught members of the IRA in possession of weapons, without opening fire on them. For instance on May 4th 1974 a four man UDR patrol from 6 UDR set up a VCP in the early hours of the morning at Trillick. When they stopped a mini with four men inside, one of the occupants tried to throw a revolver from the car into the nearby hedgerow. At this juncture the remaining occupants of the car were searched. One of whom was found to have a revolver in his jacket pocket. "Now let me see, for the man to throw the weapon he had to have it in his hand, right?"

No member of this UDR patrol opened fire on what was obviously an armed IRA active service unit on its way to commit some foul deed. Conversely the four IRA volunteers were taken captive at some considerable risk to the UDR soldiers in the patrol. If we were to listen to the republican propaganda, we would surely expect that at the first site of a weapon, a blood bath would ensue. In fact the UDR patrol showed both courage and control by taking the men captive. The men were taken to Enniskillen police station and handed over to the RUC. The outcome of which was that a joint 1RTR and police operation was set up, and later that same day we were directed to search a farm yard at Drummackan in County Fermanagh, where we found a Ford Cortina with a 500lb bomb in the boot. Further searches of the farm brought to light another two sacks of explosives, weapons, det cord and detonators, along with some ammunition. A Royal Engineers specialist search team was sent for and searched the farm house. The searches went on for three days and netted more weapons and parts. Five days later the IRA hit back at our families with another large bomb in the army married quarters.

Another instance of security forces restraint was as previously recounted, the capture of Sillery (The guy on the bomb in the photograph) and Hoben, where I was present. Even though when first sighted both these men were carrying M1 Gerand rifles no one opened fire. Instead they were run down on foot and captured by soldiers who took the risk that they may have further concealed weapons.

The numbers of similar incidents where security forces took large risks in taking captive armed IRA volunteers are numerous and if you view the Province as a whole it was a very regular occurrence. Another incident occurred when on August 10th 1974 soldiers belonging to Command Troop 1st Royal Tank Regiment were manning an OP on a border crossing near Castlederg in County Tyrone. They couldn't believe their luck when they saw two cars pull up and three armed men and one unarmed; start loading milk churns into the boot of one of the cars. Instead of opening fire on these armed volunteers the soldiers shouted a challenge to give the men chance to surrender. On hearing the challenge three of the men took off running in the direction of the Republic. Only at this point did the Command troop soldiers open fire hitting one of the terrorists in two places. Two men escaped across the border and two men were taken captive. One of the captured men turned out to be the owner of the hijacked car who was being forced at gun point to drive the vehicle to an unspecified security forces target.

If these soldiers had opened fire on the group without shouting a warning they may well have killed them all, including the man who subsequently turned out to be an innocent captive of the others. Instead they acted in a controlled and thoughtful way, and in doing so lost the chance of capturing or killing two IRA volunteers. By far the greater victory though, was achieved by them freeing unharmed the innocent man. This kind of controlled behaviour was far more prevalent throughout the army including the UDR, than the army's critics would allow.

Earlier, when the three masked and armed volunteers burst into the man's house he showed great courage by refusing to drive the vehicle for them. The consequence of this action was that he was smashed to the floor with the butt of a rifle and forced to participate or forfeit his life. The injured man, who was an IRA volunteer, was subsequently charged with possession of explosives.

The difference in treatment in the Republic between IRA suspects and persons operating on behalf of the British state was stark. Throughout the troubles, sentences such as 6 months imprisonment for membership of the IRA and little over a year for possession of explosives were the kind of sentences routinely handed out. Their efforts to stop cross border attacks into the north can only be described as pathetic to nonexistent. Yet in contrast accidental incursions into the Republic by British security forces were treated with the utmost seriousness. At the time we could have been excused for jumping to the conclusion that something very underhand and dodgy was going on. Now thirty something years later, in light of everything we know about the Irish

State's involvement. We know that something dodgy was happening.

The Irish government's collusion with the republican movement including the Provisional IRA has started to emerge in startling detail. Government ministers of the Republic were fully involved in the formation of the Provisional IRA as well as the training and arming of it. They also helped both directly and indirectly in the funding of that organisation. We need only look at the revelations of the 1971 Dublin Arms Trial, and the recent trickle of released cabinet papers to see what was going on. In spite of hundreds of murders, many cases of torture and kidnap, which were organised and executed from the south. There is no chance of a Bloody Sunday style tribunal being set up to view these matters, because there are far too many politicians, both past and present in the Republic, with blood on their hands to risk that. Over the years the government of the Republic have winged about and condemned the activities of the British Army in the north, whilst secretly supporting the actions of the IRA's murder gangs by sitting on their hands. Republicanism in Ireland traditionally runs in families. It's not only the fathers and grandfathers of these Irish politicians that have a history of political murder, but quite often the politicians themselves.

Let's take a look at Frank Aitkin who was the Irish
Deputy Premier from 1959 to 1969 when the IRA
campaign started. During the 1920s Aitkin had led
an IRA gang that was responsible for the sectarian
murders of many Protestant civilians in the north.
His victims were picked almost at random. As long
as they were Protestant that was good enough.
Aitkins led his gang of volunteers who were mostly
from Armagh and Tyrone on attacks at Camlough
and Newtownhamilton police stations as well as
their involvement in the Altnaveigh massacre,
during which seven innocent people were killed.
They were also responsible for the killings of several
soldiers and policemen. When in 1983 this nasty
piece of work died he was given a full IRA funeral.
Along with Eamon de Valera (Irish Premier) and
Sean Lemass both former IRA terrorists, he was
responsible for the start of the longest period of
instability and conflict that Ireland has ever known.

The 1971 Dublin Arms trial
If all of this wasn't enough the true position of the
Irish Government came vividly to light during the
1971 trial of Captain James Kelly, an Irish army
intelligence officer. Captain Kelly along with
Government Ministers Charles Haughey, and Neil
Blaney, both members of Jack Lynch's Fianna Fail
government at the time, were put on trial for the
import of weapons which were meant for the newly
blossoming conflict in the north. According to

evidence the government of the Republic had put aside £100,000 for the relief of families in the north who were affected by the attacks against the nationalist community which were taking place at the time. Mr Blaney and Mr Haughey without the knowledge or participation of Jack Lynch their Prime Minister, decided to channel most of this money into the purchase of arms on the European black market.

Captain Kelly had a number of meetings with different politicians about the purchase and distribution of these weapons and notably with the then Chief of Staff of the resurgent IRA Cathal Goulding, Captain Kelly claimed to be working under orders from his superior, Colonel Hefferon. It was subsequently discovered that the colonel's evidence to the court had been doctored.
All charges against Blaney were dropped before he came to trial. This left Captain Kelly and the three other defendants who consisted of a Belfast Republican, a Belgian ex-Nazi, and the soon to be Irish Prime Minister, Charles Houghey.

After a great deal of highly embarrassed political shuffling, Houghey was accused of having full knowledge of what was going on. He admitted having arranged for the passage of these weapons through customs, claiming that he knew nothing about the true nature of the shipment. The trial became even more uncomfortable for the Irish Government when Jim Gibbons, who was the Irish Defence Minister at the time of the imports, stated in evidence that Charles Houghey knew everything about the conspiracy and was in fact part of it. The conclusion of the trial was that none of the defendants were guilty.

This small window into the workings of the Republic's judicial system may help to explain why out of eighty requests for extradition that the Irish Government received from the United Kingdom between the years 1970 and 1980; a grand total of only one extradition took place. The reasons given for not handing over these 79 bombers, murderers and assassins, were usually that their crimes were political.

We are all of us products of our history and environment, and the history of the Irish Government is one of close links to, and covenant with The IRA.
For much of my life I have tried to rationalise these events, and my willing involvement in them, without, I hasten to add, complete success. My survival of those early years itself, doesn't make much sense. Maybe the gods of war were on my side. There were certainly times when it felt as if no one else was. My instinct tells me that there is no answer to my many questions, but surely there are

reasons for everything. Aren't there?

Looking back I remember my first taste of war, from the 20th November 1965 for a year to the very day. Along with many other young soldiers in my regiment, I felt the cuts of treachery, as a particularly left wing Labour government scuttled from the unpopular concept of empire. It was of course the armed forces that paid the price of the government's newly found morality, which cost us dearly, with many young men's lives.

The earlier, indecently and hasty retreat from Suez, when the Americans showed us the real meaning of the so called "Special Relationship", meant the abandonment of hundreds of tons of weapons and explosives on the quayside at Port Side, and at other places along the canal. A great deal of this equipment turned up again a few short years later to be used against us in what is now called The Yemen. Our vehicles were being blown up on our own anti tank mines, and blasted apart by our own Bazookas. The obscenity of so many British boys being killed and maimed by British weapons and ammunition appeared not to faze our political masters of either persuasion. In my humble opinion, governments should never choose war unless they are prepared to make the necessary sacrifices to win them.

A Few Facts about the Conflict in Northern Ireland.

In the years 1973 - 74 a total of 103 Soldiers, regular and UDR. & 9 police officers were killed during terrorist attacks.

In the years 1973 - 74 a total of 1031 Soldiers, regular and UDR & 263 police officers were injured in action.

In the years 1973 - 74 1663 bombs exploded in Ulster. A further 970 where neutralised by ATOs.

In 1974 there were also 270 incendiary attacks resulting in the loss of or damage to, a great deal of property.

Historical Notes Aden

In January 1964 Operation Nutcracker started in the Radfan Mountains of South Arabia. British troops fought and beat the Egyptian backed communist guerrillas. In April of the same year Operation Cap badge reasserting federal control over the whole region, by routing out any further pockets of resistance, the effects of which was to drive this opposition underground. When the new Labour Government decided to withdraw British support for our allies in the federation the rebels were suddenly in a win/win situation and the rest of the population had to scramble to align themselves with the rebel cause.

The most bloody and gallant action took place during the Aden Mutiny in June '67. The local police and Federal Regular Army in the township of Crater mutinied and killed 24 British soldiers. Their bodies were dragged through the streets and mutilated by the mutineers. The response of our political masters in London was predictably weak and cowardly. The troops were ordered to pull out and leave our fallen comrades to rot in the streets. Mad Mitch, the colonel of the Argyll and Sutherland Highlanders, decided to disobey this order and his regiment fought their way back into Crater with their bagpipes playing and quashed the revolt. Many of the mutineers were killed and a shaky kind of order was restored. Within a few months of these events Britain's role finally came to an end.

These days it is the trend to look back on empire and imperialism with embarrassment. Anyone trying to list its good points is in danger of being shouted down and labelled reactionary. Nevertheless we were part of that great empire and most of the time we made a good job of it. The South Arabian Desert is the home of some of the fiercest tribal people in the world. There, system of beliefs and traditions stretch back unbroken into history, one of the most important of these traditions is the maintenance of Face. It was and is important for these tribal warriors to only be beaten by extreme force in order for them to be able to maintain Face amongst their equals. We can be tempted to think of Arab women as downtrodden and without a voice, but if tribal warriors do not perform as expected, their women would pretty soon let them know. It was acceptable for these warriors to be beaten by extreme force without any loss of 'face', the British were acutely aware of this in their treatment of these desert tribesmen. Of course it would be completely unacceptable to inflict huge casualties on these semi nomads. So a scheme was worked out by which we were able to show awesome face saving power without causing casualties. If a village was found to be continuing helping insurgents after being warned, a leaflet drop would take place informing them that the following day at a set time the village would be destroyed by air strike and all the inhabitants were to leave the village before the appointed hour. It took only a few days to rebuild the mud houses of the village in a new location, and the ferocity of the air strike was enough to both save face for the elders and warn them to clean up their act. They usually obeyed these serious warnings and earned financial reward for good behaviour. The intention of these strikes was that none of these incredible people got hurt. The beneficial effects of aerial bombardment are a difficult concept for the modern mind to grasp, but oddly it did work. It probably saved the lives of many people, the alternative being Cordon and Search which would have ended in gun fights and collateral damage.

It is sad to reflect that many of our former enemies have now started to bitterly regret their actions against us. The port of Aden has dropped from being the third busiest in the world to being an unused backwater and the whole of the Protectorate has been swallowed up by their northern neighbour, the Yemen. There has been no peace for the people since we left. They have had to endure communism, almost constant warfare and brutal religious oppression, and more recently they find themselves the unhappy hosts to Al-Qaeda. The whole of the Gulf of Aden and the western part of the Indian Ocean have, since our leaving, become pirate infested waters and the same instability has returned that was the cause of Britain's interest in the region in 1838.

While researching this book I came across an article in the *Sunday Times* with the heading "We regret driving out the British, say Aden's former rebels." The article was dated 2010 and quotes a number of former rebels who would dearly like to turn back the clock. Their rebellion against us was stated to be a "great mistake" by one of these elderly fighters, according to the article; he added that if the British came back the rebels would sign a protocol stating that they were sorry. Another one asked himself "Why did we do it? They taught us how to live." "They" were meaning the British.

Many of the old FLOSY fighters hate their union with the Yemen and think it's the worst thing that ever happened to their country. They talk unrealistically about getting the British to come back.

I find it so incredibly sad that after fighting us for their freedom they found only more brutal chains. All those lives lost for nothing. In fact it could be argued that the power vacuum created in Southern

Arabia by the UK's abdication of its responsibilities there, may have contributed to two Gulf wars and the rise of Islamic State in the region.

Secret Soldiers: Ulster   Web site.
www.dmcevoy.com

THE MAN IN THE ARENA

It is not the critic who counts.
Nor the man who points out how
the strong man stumbles,

The credit belongs to the man
who is actually in the arena;
whose face is marred by dust
and sweat and blood;

Who knows great enthusiasm,
great devotion and the triumph
of achievement.
Or where the doer of deeds
could have done them better.

And who, at the worst, if he fails
at least fails whilst daring greatly -
so that his place shall never be
with those odd and timid souls
who know neither victory or defeat.

You've never lived until you have almost died.
For those who have had to fight for it.
Life has truly a flavour
the protected shall never know.

By Theodore Roosevelt 1910

Abbreviations

- .38: a calibre of ammunition.
- .45: a calibre of ammunition.
- ´B´ Specials: An irregular police unit with a bad reputation.
- ´B´ Vehicle: Soft skin vehicles such has trucks and Land Rovers.
- ´Q´ Car: A covert civilian type vehicles used by the army.
- 12 Bore or 12 GAGE: A shotgun calibre.
- 14 Intelligence Company: a special forces unit of the British Army that operated in Northern Ireland, United Kingdom
- 14: 14 Intelligence Company, Special Forces who operated in Northern Ireland.
- 1RTR: The First Royal Tank Regiment (The regiment fulfilled an infantry role during 1973-4)
- 4 Field Troop: Special Forces who operated in Northern Ireland.
- 4 Square Laundry: An undercover army operation which went badly wrong.

- 5th Enniskillen Dragoon Guards or 5th Skins: An Irish regiment in the British Army.
- 7.62mm: a calibre of ammunition.
- 9-milly: an informal term for 9mm.
- 9mm: a calibre of ammunition.
- Active service unit: a term for a IRA cell of several members.
- AFV: abbreviation of 'armoured fighting vehicle'.
- Aldershot: The Military Township of Aldershot is known as the home of the British Army.
- Ammunition technical officer: an army ammunitions specialist responsible for Bomb Disposal.
- ANFO: A low explosive commonly manufactured and used by the IRA for the making IEDs (bombs).
- AP: abbreviation of 'armour-piercing'.
- Armalite Rifle: American manufactured light weight assault rifle.
- ASAP: abbreviation of 'as soon as possible'.
- ASU: abbreviation of an IRA 'active service unit'.
- ATO: abbreviation of 'ammunitions technical officer'.
- Back: to come to a team member's aid.

- Bad Ammunition: Much of the weapons and ammunition used by the terrorists was stored under very poor conditions and therefore became unreliable.
- BAOR: an abbreviation of 'British Army of the Rhine'.
- Basha: an improvised shelter.
- BDU: abbreviation of 'battle dress uniform'.
- Belfast Brigade: IRA in Belfast.
- Belleek: a town in Ulster which is the most westerly point of the United Kingdom.
- bergen: a backpack carried by members of the British armed forces.
- Black Opps or (operations): Secret or undercover operations which are acted out under more relaxed rules.
- Blast Radius: The effective kill area of an explosion of any given size.
- Blowback: political fallout from afar.
- Blue on Blue: accidental friendly fire situation.
- BM: abbreviation of 'BMW'.
- Bomb Squad: Army slang for soldiers involved in making safe IEDs and other explosives.
- Brew: a cup of tea, or to prepare tea.
- British Empire Medal:

- **Canal Zone: The area around the Suez Canal.**
- **Castlederg: a small border town in county Tyrone, often suffering cross border attacks from the Irish Republic.**
- **Chicksands**: Defence Intelligence and Security Centre **and the Headquarters of the** British Army's Intelligence Corps.
- **Chopper: helicopter.**
- **CIA: abbreviation of 'Central Intelligence Agency'.**
- **CID: Criminal Investigation Department, police.**
- **Citation: An official description of the actions leading up to the awarding of a medal.**
- **City, the: the City of London in England.**
- **Civil Rights Movement: A** campaign for Social Justice in Northern Ireland dating from the early 1960s.
- **Civvies: Civilian clothing.**
- **Clogher: A small border village in county Fermanagh.**
- **close target reconnaissance: reconnaissance at very close range.**
- **CO: abbreviation of 'commanding officer'.**
- **Coffin Party: The Friends and family of the deceased, who carry the coffin at a funeral.**

- Cold War: A time after World War 2 which lasted until the fall of the Soviet Empire.
- Combatants: the sides involved in a conflict or war.
- Command Line: an electric cable used in conjunction with a battery to remotely detonate a Improvised Explosive Devise.
- Commanding officer: the officer in command of a military unit.
- Conflict: Two or more sides, groups or nations involved in an armed struggle.
- Cook off: Military Slang term, meaning ammunition or explosives going off unexpectedly.
- Cookhouse: British Army slang for the place in camp where meals are cooked and eaten.
- Co-op: A low explosive mad from animal feed sugar.
- Counter-terrorism: practices and tactics against terrorism.
- Covert Operation: a military operation carried out in secret.
- Covert: Secret and clandestine behaviour.
- CS gas: tear gas.
- CT: abbreviation of 'counter-terrorism'.
- CTR: abbreviation of 'close target reconnaissance'.

- Culvert Mine: A large amount of explosives placed in a culvert beneath a road in order to attack security forces.
- David O´Connal: (IRA Chief of staff & head of Provisional Army Council in 1973)
- Dead letter box: a location used in espionage for the anonymous transfer of items or information.
- Deep Cover Spies:
- Deniable op: an abbreviation of 'deniable operation'.
- Deniable operation: an operation that is secretly undertaken for an authority.
- Deniable operator: an operator working on a deniable operation.
- Det Cord: Detonation Cord, used either on its own or in conjunction with other explosives.
- Det: an abbreviation of 'detonation'.
- Det: 'detachment', a term for a unit of the British Army that operated in Northern Ireland, United Kingdom.
- Detonator: used to electrically initiate an explosion.
- Devil Dog or DD: A fictitious code name for a real person.
- DLB: A Dead Letter Box.
- DLB: abbreviation of 'dead letter box'.
- Double Agent: Either a spy working for both sides or pretending to work for one

side but in fact working for the opposition.

- Double tap: a shooting technique of two well-placed shots at a target in rapid succession.
- DPM: abbreviation of 'disruptive pattern material' or camouflage.
- Emirate: Ruled by a Emir (a feudal prince).
- EOD Section: an official name for Bomb Squad.
- Explosive Sniffer Dog: A dog who is part of a man / dog team, who has been trained to detect explosives and weapons.
- Extraction Team: A section of men who can be called on for help if a covert operation starts to go wrong.
- Fag: a British term for a cigarette.
- Falais Camp: A British Army camp in Little Aden, South Arabia.
- Fighting Patrol: A patrol which is capable of taking a proactive stance against any threat.
- Firing point: The position from which gun fire was directed or a remotely ignited IED was set off.
- FNU: Forename unknown.
- FOB: abbreviation of 'forward operating base'.

- Forward operating base: a secured military position
- Foxtrot: on foot
- Freds: British double agents within the IRA. Usually IRA Volunteers who have been ´ Turned ´.
- Freedom Fighter:
- FRU: Force Research Unit. A highly secret unit of the British Army.
- Fruit machines: a British English term for gaming machines
- Gamil Abdul Nasser: Egyptian President in mid 1950s.
- Garda: The Irish Republic´s police force.
- Geneva Convention:
- Gerry Adams: An IRA commander who was there leader in Belfast in the early 1970s.
- Gerrymandering: The manipulation of voting catchment areas, in order to give one party an unfair advantage during voting.
- Gillie Suit: Special sniper suit for close up camouflage.
- Good Friday Agreement: An agreement to end the conflict and work together and work together for the good of the whole community in Northern Ireland.

- **Gortin Road: The main road passing Lisanelly Camp and travelling to the centre of Omagh.**
- **GPMG: abbreviation of 'general-purpose machine gun'.**
- **Grenadier: A soldier who throws grenades and a member of a Guards regiment in the British Army.**
- **HE: an abbreviation of 'high explosive'.**
- **Hereford: a term for the Special Air Service.**
- **HMG: abbreviation of 'Her Majesty's Government'.**
- **Home goal: Military slang for terrorist who accidently kills himself whilst preparing or transporting explosives.**
- **Home Office: a department of the Government of the United Kingdom.**
- **Honey Trap:**
- **HQ Security Forces base: a generic term for a British Army base in Northern Ireland, United Kingdom during The Troubles.**
- **HQ: abbreviation of 'headquarters'.**
- **Ian Paisley: A protestant political leader.**
- **ID: abbreviation of 'identity'.**
- **IED: Improvised Explosive Device.**
- **IG: abbreviation of 'Intelligence Group'.**

- Informant: A person who gives information about terrorist activities to the security forces.
- INLA: abbreviation of 'Irish National Liberation Army'.
- Int Corps: see Intelligence Corps.
- Int: abbreviation of 'intelligence'.
- Intelligence Cell: A room or rooms where an intelligence unit works from.
- Intelligence Corps: a division of the British Army responsible for gathering military intelligence.
- Intelligence Group: a team of the Secret Intelligence Service.
- IR: abbreviation of 'infrared'.
- IRA Army Council: The joint military leadership of the Provisional IRA.
- IRA Execution: A murder committed by the Irish Republican Army in execution style, (often two bullets fired into the back of the victims head).
- IRA Volunteer: A rank within the Irish Republican Army.
- IRA: Irish Republican Army.
- Jumbiya dagger: a curved Arabian knife, worn as part of traditional dress.
- K: a term for an operator on a deniable operation.
- K: an abbreviation for 'kilometre'.

- Keeni Meeni: Under Cover operations that took place in Kenya during the Mow Mow uprising. (Swahili for "like a snake")
- Kenya: A country in East Africa.
- KF shirt: a khaki flannel shirt worn by members of the British Army.
- KF: see 'KF shirt'.
- Knife Edge: A physical barrier in a Vehicle Check Point where cars are stopped and searched.
- L
- Lisanelly Camp: A Military base and regional HQ in Omagh, County Tyron.
- Listed: to be placed on a watch list by a government.
- Little Aden: A coastal area of South Arabia, now part of The Yemen.
- London: A term for the British 'Secret Intelligence Service'.
- Long and lat: Abbreviation of 'longitude and latitude'.
- M1 Rifle: Obsolete US Army.
- Ma salaam: Arabic for good bye.
- Married Quarters: An area of housing where soldier's families live.
- Martin McGuiness:
- Mau-Mau: A vicious terrorist group in 1950s Kenya.

- MI5: Civilian intelligence and counter espionage organisation working mainly within the United Kingdom.
- MI6: An obsolete but popular term for the Secret Intelligence Service.
- MI6: Civilian intelligence and counter espionage organisation working mainly outside the United Kingdom.
- Mid Ulster Brigade: A collection of active service units of the IRA, Operating in the southern part of Ulster during the recent IRA campaign.
- Mini Clubman: small car of UK manufacture, a variant of the Mini.
- Ministry of Defence: a department of the Government of the United Kingdom.
- MIO: Military Intelligence Officer.
- Misfire: When a weapon fails to fire correctly.
- MoD: abbreviation of 'Ministry of Defence'.
- MOE: abbreviation of 'method of entry'.
- Mortar: A tubular shaped weapon that directs a rocket propelled explosive charge with a high trajectory.
- MPV: abbreviation of 'multi-purpose vehicle'.
- MRF: abbreviation of ´Military Reconnaissance Force´.

- NAAFI: Navy, Army, Air, Force, Association, (similar to US PX).
- NATO: abbreviation of 'North Atlantic Treaty Organization'.
- NHS: abbreviation of 'National Health Services'.
- Nightsun: a searchlight, used by police helicopters.
- NORAID (Irish Northern Aid Committee): an Irish-American fundraising body.
- NORAID: An organisation used by the IRA to collect money for the purchase of weapons in the United States.
- Normal Vetting: A standard level of security vetting.
- North Atlantic Treaty Organization: an intergovernmental military alliance.
- Northern Ireland/Ulster:
- Northern Ireland: The northern part of the island of Ireland which is part of Great Briton. (Ulster)
- NV: Normal Vetting.
- NVG: abbreviation of 'night viewing goggles' or 'night vision goggles
- Observation Post: A place where you can covertly watch terrorist suspects.
- Official Secrets Act: legislation that provides for the protection of state secrets and official information.
- OP: Observation Post.

- Operations officer: An officer responsible for standard military operations.
- Operations room (ops room): a room in which operations are managed.
- Operator: a soldier in a Special Forces team or paramilitary group.
- Ops Room: an operations room.
- Ops Room: Operations Room.
- OPSEC: abbreviation of 'operational security'.
- Orange Hall: A community hall built and controlled by members of the Orange Order.
- OTR: abbreviation of 'on the run'.
- Palestine: An area of the Middle East.
- Pass number: an identification number between undercover parties.
- PE: abbreviation of 'plastic explosive'.
- PE4: British manufactured plastic explosive.
- Permanent cadre: an ongoing appointment.
- Peter Flanagan: An inspector in the RUC who was murdered by the IRA.
- PIRA: abbreviation of 'Provisional Irish Republican Army'.
- Plain Cloths: The wearing of civilian clothing in order not be recognised as a soldier.

- Player: a person involved in the collection of intelligence data and a player in the Game.
- Players: People involved in ´ The Game ´.
- Pongo: Navy slang term for soldier.
- Positive vetting: a higher level security assessment.
- POW: abbreviation of 'prisoner of war'.
- Prod or (Protestant) paramilitary: members of Protestant terrorist groups.
- Provisional Irish Republican Army: Irish republican paramilitary organisation.
- Provos: Army slang for members of the Provisional IRA.
- Provos: members of the Provisional IRA.
- Pseudo-Gangs: British led paramilitary forces who fought against the Mow Mow during their uprising.
- PTSD: Post Traumatic Stress Disorder, common amongst soldiers after experiencing combat.
- PV: Positive Vetting.
- QRF: abbreviation of 'quick reaction force'.
- Quartermaster: An officer in charge of stores.
- R&R: military slang for 'rest and recuperation'.
- Radfan: An area of South Arabia now part of the Yemen where the British forces

fought a military campaign in the early 1960s.

- RC: Roman Catholic.
- Recce: abbreviation of 'reconnaissance'.
- Red Hand Commandos: A secretive Protestant paramilitary group.
- Red Hand of Ulster: a symbol to denote the province of Ulster.
- Regiment: a term for the Special Air Service.
- Republic of Yemen: A country in the southern part of Arabia.
- Rhino: a very large sea going raft, of World War 2 American manufacture. Used for transporting military vehicles from ship to shore during operations.
- RHQ: abbreviation of 'regimental headquarters'.
- RPG 7: Russian rocket propelled grenade, fired from a hand held launcher.
- RPG: abbreviation of 'rocket-propelled grenade'.
- RUC: abbreviation of 'Royal Ulster Constabulary'.
- Rupert: a term for a young officer.
- RV: abbreviation of 'rendezvous'.
- Safety blanket: another term for a security blanket.
- Saint Angelo: a large fortified military compound to the north of Enniskillen.

- SAS: abbreviation of 'Special Air Service'.
- Sat comms: an abbreviation of 'satellite communications'.
- SB: abbreviation of Special Branch.
- SDLP: Social Democratic Labour Party, mainly Catholic.
- Sectarian: Violence and hatred between members of different religions within a community.
- Security service: an alias of the Secret Intelligence Service.
- Security survey:
- Segmented Plate: A device which was used to disrupt IEDs (bombs)in the early nineteen seventies.
- Selection: the selection procedure for Special Forces.
- Semtex: Check manufactured plastic explosive.
- SF: abbreviation of 'Special Forces'.
- Sheikdom: A country ruled by a feudal Sheik.
- Shin fain: The political wing of the IRA.
- SIS: abbreviation of 'Secret Intelligence Service'.
- Sit Rep: an abbreviated form of 'situation report'.
- slime: a term for the Intelligence Corps.
- Slot: to kill.

- Small Wars: The numerous smaller conflicts all over the world that British forces were involved in.
- Snoopers: A derogatory term used by republicans for soldiers involved in intelligence gathering.
- SNU: Surname unknown.
- SOP: abbreviation of 'standard operating procedure'.
- South Arabia: A British protectorate which is now part of the Yemen.
- Soviet Union: a term for the 'Union of Soviet Socialist Republics'.
- Special Air service: a Special Forces division of the British Army.
- Special Branch: a term for special units of police forces with national security responsibilities.
- Special Forces: special units of armed forces.
- Squaddie: a term for a British soldier.
- Standard operating procedure: the accepted steps and activities to conduct a process or procedure.
- STDs: Sexually Transmitted Disease.
- Steak Knife:
- Stickie: Belfast slang for a local IRA volunteer.

- **Stopping point:** The place in a Vehicle Check Point where cars are stopped and searched.
- **Stormont:** Stormont Castle, the seat of the Northern Ireland Assembly.
- **Sue Helicopter:** A small helicopter with a Perspex bubble front, used for recon purposes and transport.
- **Suez Crisis: A** military confrontation between British, French and the Egyptians' in 1956.
- **SWAT: abbreviation of 'special weapons and tactics'**
- **T**
- **T34: a World War 2 Russian tank.**
- **Tab: a British Army term for a loaded march.**
- **Tanky: A member of The Royal Tank Regiment, also of other units of the Armoured Corp who are currently on tanks.**
- **TAVR or TA: Territorial Army Volunteer Reserve, part time units of British Army.**
- **Terrorists: Someone using violence to gain political aims.**
- **The Deanery: This old Deanery in the village of Clogher was used by the army as an HQ for a UDR company and by 1RTR as a patrol base. The largest single IRA**

attack of the whole campaign occurred there on May the 2nd 1974.

- The Enclave: Military slang for an area of the Irish Republic including the town of Monaghan which is surrounded on three sides by Northern Ireland and was used by the IRA for committing a constant stream of cross border attacks.
- The Firm: the British Secret Intelligence Service.
- The Game: An in word for the Intelligence world (believed to have come from Britons involvement in the Afghan Wars of 19th century)
- The Gathering: The author's description of the soldiers and police officers who normally attended the scene of a major incident.
- The Iron Curtain: A mainly imaginary barrier dividing east and west Europe after World War 2.
- The North: Northern Ireland or Ulster.
- The Orange Order: A mainly Protestant political organisation.
- The Republic: The Irish Republic.
- The Republican Movement: A political and military grouping that bereaved Ulster should become part of the Irish Republic.

- **The Service:** a term for the British Secret Intelligence Service.
- **The Troubles:** Different periods during modern Irish history when the IRA have fought against both the British and the Irish Republic's security forces.
- **UDA:** abbreviation of 'Ulster Defence Association'.
- **UFF:** Ulster Freedom Fighters, a Protestant Paramilitary Force.
- **UK:** abbreviation of 'United Kingdom'.
- **Under Cover:** Soldiers who are operationally hiding their military allegiance.
- **United States:** abbreviation of 'United States of America'.
- **Urban Camouflage:**
- **US:** abbreviation of 'United States of America'.
- **USA:** abbreviation of 'United States of America'.
- **USSR:** Abbreviation of 'Union of Soviet Socialist Republics'.
- **UVA:** Abbreviation of 'ultraviolet A light'.
- **UVF:** Ulster Volunteer Force, a Protestant Paramilitary Force.
- **Vauxhall:** A term for the Secret Intelligence Service.
- **VCP:** an abbreviation of 'vehicle checkpoint'.

- **War: A conflict which has been legally declared as a war under the rules of the Geneva Convention.**
  Wheelbarrow: The world's first bomb disposal robot.

Thanks to a few people for their help

Ness T
Sue Frog
Roy S
Sandra W
Marion M
For helping proof my manuscript.

Stephen J
For help with photographs.

John M
For artwork.

John T for his efforts on my behalf.

Ken Ma & Michael Me
To whom I owe special thanks.

14511249R00209

Printed in Great Britain
by Amazon.co.uk, Ltd.,
Marston Gate.